Affirmative Aging

Affirmative Aging
A *Creative* Approach to *Longer* Life
New Edition

Edited by
Joan E. Lukens

for

The Episcopal Society for Ministry on Aging, Inc.

MOREHOUSE PUBLISHING
Harrisburg, PA

Morehouse Publishing
P.O. Box 1321
Harrisburg, PA 17105

Library of Congress Cataloging-in-Publication Data
Affirmative aging: a creative approach to longer life / edited by Joan E. Lukens; for the
Episcopal Society for Ministry on Aging, Inc. — New ed.
     p.   cm.
Includes bibliographical references.
ISBN 0-8192-1623-2
     1. Aged—Religious life.   I. Lukens, Joan E.   II. Episcopal Society for Ministry
on Aging, Inc.   (U.S.)
BV4580.A435   1994   94-18307
248.8'5—dc20   CIP

The Scripture texts in this publication are from the New Revised Standard Version
of the Bible, copyright 1989 by the Division of Christian Education of the
National Council of the Churches of Christ in the U.S.A.

Printed in the United States of America

Contents

Contributors vii

Preface
Joan E. Lukens xi

Introduction
Emma Lou Benignus xiii

How to Use This Book
Linda L. Grenz xix

Aging: A Spiritual Journey
T. Herbert O'Driscoll 1

Ethics and the Third Age
Charles J. Fahey 12

Challenge to Ministry: Opportunities for Older Persons
Emma Lou Benignus 23

Meditation and Prayer
Nancy Roth 41

The Gift of Wisdom
Robert W. Carlson 58

Intergenerational Relationships: Adult Children and Aging Parents
Helen Kandel Hyman 72

The Church as Family
JoAnn S. Jamann-Riley 88

Toward Creative Aging: The Church's Response
Karen Johnson Karner 98

Death Preparation as Life Enhancement
Eugene C. Bianchi 112

Further Reading
Henry C. Simmons 135

Chapter Study Guides
Linda L. Grenz and Lynn W. Huber . . . . Following each chapter

The Episcopal Society for Ministry on Aging, Inc., is a national resource for the Episcopal Church for developing ministries with and on behalf of older persons. ESMA works through denominational, interfaith, and societal networks to serve the needs of spirit, mind, and body of the aging and promotes their continued contribution to church and society, maximizing their unique gifts and talents.

This resource was funded in part by the Adult Education and Leadership Development Office of the Episcopal Church.

The Episcopal Society for Ministry on Aging, Inc.
323 Wyandotte Street
Bethlehem, PA 18015-1527

Phone: (610) 868-5400
Fax: (610) 691-1682

Contributors

Emma Lou Benignus, an Episcopalian, has studied in philosophy, theology, spirituality, adult education, and gerontology. She was professor of pastoral theology at the Episcopal Theological Seminary (now Episcopal Divinity School), taught religion at Randolph-Macon College and Columbia's College of General Studies, and has written many articles. She has worked with churches in America, Europe, and Africa and has directed the national aging program for the American Baptist Church. Her focus now is on the spiritual growth of the elderly.

Eugene C. Bianchi, professor of religion at Emory University, is the author of *Aging as a Spiritual Journey* (Crossroad, 1982) and *On Growing Older* (Crossroad, 1985). In addition to conducting conferences and workshops on aging and human development, Dr. Bianchi has written a new book, *Elder Wisdom: Crafting Your Own Elderhood* (Crossroad, 1994), based on 105 interviews with creative elders. His other books and articles range widely over religious, cultural, and psychological issues.

The Rev. Robert W. Carlson, Ph.D., has recently retired after 40 years of full-time ministry, which included 22 years in parish work, 11 years of teaching at Seabury-Western Theological Seminary, and 7 years as a diocesan staff member. His interest in the field of aging began early in parish ministry with the discovery of the rich resource of wisdom found in elderly members. A course he taught in seminary brought together an equal number of traditional students and older persons to engage issues of ministry with and to older persons. He is the author of the Episcopal Church's 1994 *Age in Action* material and other articles and reviews on aging. In his retirement years he hopes to "pursue wisdom" and to continue work in research and writing.

Msgr. Charles J. Fahey is a parish priest, social activist, public speaker, and innovator. As a teacher and administrator, particularly at Fordham University's Third Age Center, where he is a senior associate and the Marie Ward Doty Professor of Aging Studies, he has fostered a climate of study and research that has led to new insights into aging-related issues. During his tenure, the center has become an important national resource for research, education, and training. As a public speaker he has been an advocate for those in the third age. He has worked to improve long-term care and housing for the elderly. He has played a major role in stimulating and helping religious groups in their activities for older persons. Msgr. Fahey has served as a board member and president of both the National Conference of Catholic Charities and the American Association of Homes for the Aging. He was a member of the working group on ethics for the National Task Force on Health Care Reform. He was a charter member of the Federal Council on Aging, having been appointed by Presidents Nixon, Ford and Carter, the latter of whom selected him as chairman. He is president of the American Society on Aging, a fellow of the Gerontological Society of America, a fellow of the Institute of Medicine of the National Academy of Science, and a fellow of the New York Academy of Medicine.

The Rev. Linda L. Grenz, an Episcopal priest, has served as coordinator for adult education and leadership development of the Episcopal Church. She assembled and edited *In Dialogue with Scripture: An Episcopal Guide to Studying the Bible* and developed the *Discipleship Group*, manuals for small group ministry in the Episcopal Church. She is president of LeaderResources (1116 West 8th Street, Wilmington, DE 19806). LeaderResources produces customized training manuals and leader's guides to equip the saints. It also offers consulting services and conferences to judicatories and congregations in leadership development.

Lynn W. Huber, Ph.D., ACSW, a gerontologist and social worker, was educated at Barnard College, Hunter College School of Social Work, and Case Western Reserve University. She directed the Social Work Program at Edinboro University in Pennsylvania and offered continuing education courses at the Church Divinity School of the Pacific and the School of Theology at the University of the South. Dr. Huber was the director of the model older adult ministry program for the Episcopal Diocese of Tennessee. She offers workshops, courses, retreats, and consultation for congregations and judicatories, as well as spiritual direction for individuals and groups. She edited the Diocese of Tennessee's quarterly newsletter, *Aging Is Becoming*, and has published articles in journals and in the *Handbook on Religion, Spirituality and Aging* (forthcoming from Fortress Press).

Helen Kandel Hyman began her career as a radio script writer at CBS and later, after moving to Connecticut, became a free-lance writer and editor. Her books include *A Treasury of the World's Greatest Fairy Tales*, (Grolier, 1972) and with Dr. Barbara Silverstone, *You and Your Aging Parent* (Pantheon Books, 1976, revised 1982 and 1989). The latter was a Consumers Union Book Selection. Silverstone and Hyman are also coauthor's of *Growing Older Together* (Pantheon Books, 1992).

JoAnn S. Jamann-Riley, E.D.D., is professor emeritus, Columbia University, and an Oblate of the Order of John the Baptist. As a nurse-educator, Dr. Riley practiced in hospitals and community agencies, developed graduate programs in nursing, led many conferences, and served as a national and international consultant. Her clinical specialty is gerontological nursing. Following retirement from the academic setting, she initiated a Ministry in Health and Aging at the Cathedral Church of the Nativity, Bethlehem, Pennsylvania. Currently, she lives in rural South Carolina where she serves as a home health nurse, vestry member, and literacy tutor.

Karen Johnson (Panayotoff) Karner, E.D.D, is professor of nursing at East Stroudsburg University, East Stroudsburg, Pennsylvania, where she served as the founding coordinator for the university's Gerontology Concentration Program (1989-1992). Dr. Karner is a consultant, as a clinical specialist in gerontological nursing, and serves on the Committee on Aging for the Episcopal Church in the Diocese of Bethlehem, Pennsylvania. She has published on such topics as pain management in older adults, continuing education, and the health of older adults. Dr. Karner is a member of the Prince of Peace Evangelical Lutheran Church in Johnsonville, Pennsylvania, where she assists in the planning of adult educational activities.

Joan E. Lukens, executive secretary of the Episcopal Society for Ministry on Aging, Inc. (ESMA) since 1987, is its only full-time employee. In this capacity, with the board, she administers the Episcopal Church's national program on aging. She is the editor of the new edition of *Affirmative Aging*. She developed and edits ESMA's newsletter, *ESMA's*

Network News. A graduate of Salem College, Winston-Salem, North Carolina, in sociology and elementary education, most of her career has been devoted to professional lay work for the Episcopal Church, as a Diocese of Bethlehem staff member and with the Rev. Charles R. Wilson, CRW Management Services.

Herbert O'Driscoll, a native of Ireland, is rector of Christ Church (Anglican) in Calgary, Alberta. He has served parishes in Ireland and Canada and has been a chaplain in the Royal Canadian Navy and warden of the College of Preachers at Washington Cathedral, Washington, D.C. He has spoken extensively in the United States and Canada and written hymns, radio and television scripts, and nine books.

Nancy Roth is an Episcopal priest, teacher, and author. She draws on her background in theology, music, and dance in offering retreats and workshops for all ages throughout the United States and in England, with an emphasis on integration of body and spirit. Her books include *A New Christian Yoga* (Cowley, 1989); *We Sing of God: a Hymnal for Children* (edited with Robert N. Roth, Church Hymnal Corporation, 1989); *The Breath of God: An Approach to Prayer* (Cowley, 1990); *Praying: A Book for Children* (Church Hymnal Corporation, 1991), and *Organic Prayer: Cultivating Your Relationship with God* (Cowley, 1993).

Henry C. Simmons is professor of religion and aging at the Presbyterian School of Christian Education, where he also is the director of the Center on Aging. He joined the school's faculty in 1985. Previously, he taught at the Toronto School of Theology at the University of Toronto and at Garrett-Evangelical Theological Seminary in Evanston, Illinois. He holds a Ph.D. in psychology and religion from the University of Ottawa, Canada. Simmons is past president of the Religious Education Association of the United States and Canada. He is a member of the Board of Directors of the National Council on Aging, where he serves on the public policy committee and is chair of the humanities committee. He is a member of the executive committee of the board of directors of the National Interfaith Coalition on Aging, where he chairs the curriculum advisory committee for the National Clergy Leadership Project to Prepare for an Aging Society, a project funded by the Administration on Aging. He is also review editor of the *Journal of Religious Gerontology*. His ongoing research interests include spirituality and aging, and educational ministry with adults and older adults.

Preface

Aging is a natural part of life that begins with birth and ends with death. It is a process of becoming filled with the richness of experience, education, challenge, opportunity . . . the blessing of family, friends, mankind—made in God's image and His own forever . . . faith . . . growing and changing—sometimes adapting as we progress with our biopsychosocial and spiritual selves through Erikson's "stages of man" . . . drawing closer to our end and the beginning of eternity . . . an agelessness that supersedes that which **was** for that which **is**.

This was my philosophy of aging written in response to an assignment in an introductory aging course—perhaps one of the most significant assignments in my educational career. Thinking about how I would frame my philosophy led me to assess my values, beliefs, and life. Today I know that aging is God's gift to us—the gift of our life span. Aging is a process of running toward rather than running from. It is all of the process of living, moving, and having our being. As we prepare in youth for life, in the living of life we prepare for the transition that comes at life's end.

Aging is the commonality that cuts across all conditions of humanity: race, sexuality, culture, sickness, health, wealth, poverty, education, ignorance, faith, faithlessness, and so on. No matter what our composition, we are born and we die. We can be intentional, however, in how we live our lives.

The Episcopal Society for Ministry on Aging, Inc. (ESMA) has prepared this new edition of *Affirmative Aging* to develop the premise that as one ages (lives) one may learn to age affirmatively because of and in spite of the conditions of our humanity. *Affirmative Aging* is meant to unlock the chains that bind us to negative societal concepts of aging and create an awareness of the potential that can be part of our aging if we, individually and corporately, so choose. As ESMA's Age in Action materials proclaim, "Aging is becoming aware of God's grace, gifts and time."

This book on spirituality and aging is a resource for individuals, families, and for church and society. A study guide at the end of each chapter makes it possible for the reader to engage in personal reflection or for the book to be used in group study. Perhaps the final "assignment" might be to write your own or your church's philosophy of aging. Goals to serve as touchstones for occasional review would help us monitor our progress as we live into our philosophy of aging.

As the Episcopal Church's national agency on aging for 30 years, ESMA offers this book to raise the church's consciousness of its obligation to be proactive throughout the entire life span. God invites us to embrace life fully, to reach our potential, and to discover what life—and indeed older life—can be.

Acknowledgments

First we wish to give credit to all who were involved in preparing the original edition of *Affirmative Aging*—the cornerstone for this new edition. Several of the group process study guides are based on those in the original text which were developed by Julie Armstrong and Frances Reynolds Johnson.

In paying tribute to all who made this edition possible, special praise and thanks go to the authors and to ESMA's dedicated volunteer, Gabriele C. Whittier, who entered the manuscript on her computer and managed its progress through many drafts.

We are grateful to the *Affirmative Aging* editorial board, Emma Lou Benignus, the Rev. Canon Clifford B. Carr, the Rev. Linda L. Grenz, Karen Johnson Karner, E.E.D., R. Mark LaRose, and consultant Bernard E. Nash, Ph.D., for its guidance, and to Allen Kelley, president and publisher, Morehouse Publishing, and his staff.

Our sincere thanks to all who read the manuscripts and who gave of themselves in making the 30th anniversary edition of *Affirmative Aging* a reality.

Joan E. Lukens, Editor
for the Episcopal Society for Ministry on Aging, Inc.

Introduction

Emma Lou Benignus

Affirmative Aging! This book is an endorsement of the whole-life process, God's gift of time whereby each of us has opportunity through precious years for "journey into wholeness," into God.

Each of us is nudged by the life-force within to become the person we are given the capacity to be—that self whose gradual process of becoming is his or her avenue into God, the Source, the Self from whence we come, in Whom we are invited to live our life with increasing fullness and freedom until God claims us totally.

We are made in God's image. Throughout our years we are given opportunity to explore and discern this relatedness, and in that process we discover bit by bit the fullness of our own being. The journey from birth to death is now believed for many to be to a hundred, even a hundred and ten years—a wondrous stretch of time for us to experience God, to learn to "opt for God," to choose God's way, to desire God, to cooperate with God in a society that constantly beckons us elsewhere.

When we were baptized into Christ it was the Spirit, through others, who brought us there. When we were confirmed we made our own commitment, but scarcely sensing the Spirit who was luring us. Thereafter came the years of ever fuller participation in society's orderings, new tensions, unexpected demands, responsibilities sometimes staggering, with the self at high risk of losing sight of that One to whom we really belong. When the years of pressured ego-inflation finally are let go, our insights and questions find freedom to change: the old familiar "Who am I?" can now become "Whose am I?" and "To whom do I really belong?"

The authors of this book believe the poet's words that, indeed, "the last *is* that for which the first was made" and that the last of our years is a time of special freedom for journey into deep relationship with our Creator, Sustainer, Lover, God. For the riches of this journey we affirm and thank God for the gift of aging.

In 1964 at its General Convention, the Episcopal Church sanctioned the birth of the Episcopal Society for Ministry on Aging (ESMA) to serve the church as its mentor and resource on issues of aging. ESMA was empowered to study society's changing age profile and to identify implications for subsequent changes in the church's ministry with, by, and for older adults.

Now, three decades later, only a few churches report that they have actually identified their age profile, or that they have tracked the age shift as it becomes evident in their congregations. Indubitably, the changing age-composition of society will be reflected in the age-composition of the local church. To wish it otherwise is futile and to ignore it is irresponsible.

In the United States three concurrent powerful social forces are merging: the senior boom, the birth dearth, and the aging of the baby-boomers. The coming together of these three population streams will create a wide-scale demographic shift, referred to by population analyst Ken Dychtwald as the *Age Wave*. The wave is expected to peak after 2025 when the baby-boomers turn 65. At that time Americans over 65 are predicted to outnumber teenagers by more than two to one, and the median age will be 50.

If we are to cope with society's aging, we need to understand it. Just what is aging? And who are the aging? Paraphrasing Bernard Nash:

Aging—is a lifelong *process* about which everyone needs to become knowledgeable because much can be done to assure good health and vigor into later life. We age from birth to death, and every stage has its imperatives and gifts. The acceptance of one's self, one's strength and limitations, usually increases with age. *Interaction* with others and *spiritual fulfillment* are necessary to help us realize our fullest potential. Certainly the church is unique in being able to foster both of these essentials.

Age—is a *stage* of being, a stage in the aging process. Age is experienced by every person, in different ways, and differently in different times. Every stage is meant to "bring its own reward," and it will when attitudes are positive and if the environment is supportive.

The Aged—distinctly individual personae, include everyone of us, recipients and givers (contributors) in life's processes. Said Nash, "In our experience we find that the churches need to become much more knowledgeable about how to assist us with the issues of mid-life, with retirement decisions and the retirement years, and certainly with the really aged in harvesting and sharing the genius of the final experiences of life." For the most part the riches of the last years go unidentified in our youth-oriented, gerontophobic (fear of aging) society.[1]

These three meanings of *age* refer to significantly different stages and experiences, each with its own qualities, needs, and opportunities. As Christians we are meant to discern and respond to the Spirit's presence in every stage of our years whatever the circumstance. Have *we* really been taught to *discern* the Spirit's presence in the daily rounds of our ordinary lives?

Contributors to the chapters in *Affirmative Aging* all believe that the Christian community, called together by the power of God's Spirit to reveal and share that power in our ever-changing society, does have responsibility to carry a vital role in the extensive social changes that lie ahead in this new era. It is all too easy, especially in the presence of physical disabilities, to assume that "the elderly have had their day" and henceforth expect that they have nothing to contribute to the social good. Are our leaders, clergy and lay, discerning and responsive to the changing profile of their specific congregations?

When our evaluation of "old" is based primarily on the physical component of our humanness, we find ourselves out of step with the insights of developmental psychologists such as Maslow, Erikson, and Jung. In all of their research and writings, people of older years are recognized for the unique and valuable contributions they can make as they learn to respect their life experiences and honor them as ground for discerning life's truths. As Christians we believe that the Holy Spirit is always present, wherever it is we "live and move and have our being," beckoning us, as did Jesus, to "come and see," to take note of what is happening here, now, implicit in *this* situation, in *this* relationship, in *this* encounter, to discern the meaning of this moment. Who more than the "retired" have "discretionary time" and freedom to be present in the social matrix, trying to see things as God would have them be seen, free at last to be on God's track with joy and abandon, to try to comprehend life's situations in God's way? We offer several illustrations of "aging freedom" abroad in the world:

After government restrictions ended the production of Agent Orange, the lethal product used in the Vietnam War, several senior members of a congregation wondered about the disposition of the manufacturer's old inventory. To find out, they each bought some stock so as to be able to attend the stockholders meeting. There they bided their time to ask some questions, which turned out to be a distinct "embarrassment and inconvenience" for the company officials. As could be expected, some who were present were angered, but others applauded and thanked the seniors for this rightful exposure.

Another incident was reported by two older women, neighbors, who noted that their cars were sprayed during the night by debris, which they assumed was spewed from the smokestack of a nearby factory, supposedly closed. They requested the cooperation of the local newspaper and begin to investigate. Persistence eventually disclosed an illicit, clandestine affiliation between the little local plant and a distant parent corporation already faced with government closure and penalties.

In a different vein, we recall the account of three quite elderly women, bored in retirement, who said that although they could no longer house-sit active 3-year-olds, they could rock to sleep a restless baby. They offered their services to an adjacent church, which responded by opening a nursery for the newborn of single mothers, the first of its kind in the city.

As we consider the potential of our old-age freedom, we are reminded of the leaders who were called to the fore in our Hebrew-Christian history, all surprised by the "summons": Moses, Aaron, Miriam, all in their 80s, Abraham at 75, Sarah presumably beyond child-bearing, Zachariah and Elizabeth getting on in years, Simeon grown old waiting for the Savior, and Anna, long-cloistered in the Temple, at 84 heralding the newborn babe in the streets of Jerusalem! Clearly, age was no impediment for those whose hearts were open to the nudgings of the Spirit within and whose ears were open to the life around them.

The role and situation of the elderly in contemporary society was discussed for two weeks by 122 nations at the 1982 United Nations World Conference on Aging in Vienna. The position and "argument" that claimed our hearts is stated in a paper issued at that time by the Global Education Associates, *Aging and World Order*, addressed to all, especially society's elders, who want to be involved in "creating humanizing alternatives." The focus was on the special role of older people, described as "living links between the cultural and spiritual wellsprings of the past and the needs of the future." It was noted that many of the elders had learned how to live in harmony with the earth and in simple humanness, and thereby "they know the value of what is vital in shaping the future." What is needed, though, "is more confidence by older people in their own power and the will to become active agents in creating the future." It was noted that the needed power will not be realized by the elderly in isolation: "It will be realized in joining hands—old and young—forming coalitions and working together with people of all ages."

What entity in our society is better suited for this than the churches —multigenerational, male and female, potentially multicultural and multiracial, rich and poor, large and small, urban and rural? One experience all have in common is the experience of aging, and the gains and losses that come with every decade from birth to death.

We need each other but we also need *time alone*. To be ready to respond creatively to the vicissitudes of later life we need time alone for prayer, but also time alone to relive portions of our lives, to glean stored wisdom. Recollection will surface our lives' shares of suffering and joys. As we look at the past from the vantage point of new learning and deepened understanding, we recognize our capacity for appreciating an old experience in dimensions we did not—could not—see before. Such can be the deep wonderment of our own creative aging. This experience of reassessing the past is one of the enriching aspects of aging, the "ground" of the gift of wisdom.

Significant societal changes brought about by aging are in the offing. Not least is the nature of the Social Security system itself. In 1935 the system started with 40 workers contributing to one person's pension. By the year 2020 this ratio is expected to be 1.78 to 1. Today older Americans receive more benefits than younger Americans from all sources, a situation that cannot endlessly prevail. A redefinition of financial resources will occur, with the new financial measurement being wealth, not income. This, however, is precisely what the founders of the Social Security system rejoiced in being able to avoid.

What lies ahead calls for much depth of understanding and reconciliation. One hopes the senior members of the churches will be a healing presence. As the later years of life give opportunity for each person to become more individualized, more him- or herself, as we live more healthfully through our extended lifetime (many into their 90s and 100s, and in quite good form) it is hoped that the elderly themselves will help our culture break free of its gerontophobic aspects.[2]

Notes

1. For some definitions and recommendations, we turn to a paper written for the Episcopal Church by Bernard E. Nash, Ph.D., former president of ESMA, and a former executive director of the American Association of Retired Persons, in *Jubilee*, Summer 1985, Vol. 2, No. 3.

2. This is a dream that hinges on the contributions and creativity of society's elders, who will have many occasions to reveal and share the gifts of their years.

How to Use This Book

This book is a compilation of articles, each followed by two study guides. The first guide can be used as a reflection guide for an individual reader or as discussion questions for a study group. The second guide is designed for groups to engage the material experientially, to learn from themselves and each other as much as from the material presented.

The study guides are based on the following premises:

- Adults learn best when they are actively engaged in the learning process and their own life experience is honored in that learning process.

- Self-discovered learnings have more meaning and lasting effect than merely acquired information.

- It is possible for individuals within a group to learn things that are new and valuable when group members talk about their experiences; what helped or hindered them?

- Group leaders, lay or ordained, need a spirit of openness and adventure more than any specific expertise in subject matter. The leaders' role is to guide the process rather than convey information.

- Group members need to read the chapters before each session. The sessions can be used as a series for a group, or specific chapters can be used by a decision-making or special interest group. Sessions can be expanded or contracted to fit time boundaries.

- It is imperative for all participants to read each chapter prior to the study session that follows it.

This book is for those who are searching and seeking their own spiritual potential, as well as for those who are committed to a ministry for and by older persons. The book is a tool. It invites readers to consider the variety of ways in which life-styles, environments, and attitudes affect their developing spiritual lives over the years. It is designed to challenge individuals and congregations to private and corporate action.

The study guides provide formats for exploring the basic issues of each chapter. They can be used by individuals or with groups such as the following:

• Christian Education Groups: group study for better understanding of the educational needs of older adults; resource materials for educational programs, older adult groups, and intergenerational groups; background material for group leaders.

• Social Action/Outreach Groups: group study to consider how environments and activities affect spiritual well-being; for use in nursing home ministries and in other programs for the frail elderly.

• Pastoral Care Groups: a **must** for volunteers and other personnel, especially the chapters on spiritual development and death preparation.

• Pastoral Concern Groups: program resources for adult children/aging parent groups; aging parent/adult children groups; groups for caregivers of frail elderly.

• Life Review and/or Spiritual Discernment Groups: groups of older adults seeking spiritual growth; groups facing personal loss or death; groups dealing with the loss or death of significant others.

Affirmative Aging as a Springboard for Group Life Review and Discernment.

Many people have used the first edition of *Affirmative Aging* as the basis for working on their own spiritual journeys. It has been our experience that for most people, spiritual growth is encouraged best in the context of a group. The nature and style of the group may vary enormously, but certain elements seem essential:

• Members know their confidences will not be betrayed; what they say will not come back as a weapon to be used against them.

- Members share a commitment to exploring a spiritual path. (This is *not* the norm in our society, which inhibits conversation on this subject.)

- Members give each other permission to call them to account. For this confrontation to be helpful, it must be based on a sure and certain knowledge that all members truly want the best for each other and are there for the growth of all. (For example, if I say that I want to be closer to God, but acknowledge that I am not praying, someone might point out that prayer is a pretty good way to get closer to God, and gently suggest that I might want to try it.)

- Members always have permission to pass, rather than respond.

- Members speak in "I messages," based on their own experience, rather than "you messages" or "should messages," which judge others' experience. "I feel," "I hope," and "I experienced things this way" are good ways to begin "I messages."

Intergenerational Opportunities

Msgr. Charles Fahey (a contributor to this volume) says that "the future of the church is in the hands of its elders." By this he is *not* referring to changing demographics. He is referring to the fact that if the elders (or "wisdom people") show by their lives and words and faces that God has been the most important reality in their lives, and that the church is the place where their faith has been formed and nurtured, then the church is credible with middle-aged and younger people. If, on the other hand, elders drop out, they give the message that the church is a social club, not unlike the Kiwanis, useful but not important for its own sake.

This book can be used to form intergenerational groups, which benefit both old and young, to study these important issues and to share reactions and life experiences. It can also be used to help congregations develop creative intergenerational programming. Keep this in mind throughout your use of the book, even where we do not explicitly recommend intergenerational activities. You may come up with some creative ideas of your own.

Setting Ground Rules for Your Group

Before your group begins to study *Affirmative Aging*, you may want to spend some time working out an agreement about what you hope to get out of the experience, and setting some ground rules for your time together. You might include the following ideas, which we have found helpful to groups in the past:

• Start and end on time.

• Meet in a setting that will be comfortable for everyone in the group. (If you choose someone's home, consider having others provide the refreshments so the event does not become burdensome for the host.)

• Know in advance how long your group will last, and whether it will be open (new members may come at any time) or closed (the group makes a contract to meet only with ongoing members). The advantages of the latter choice is that deeper relationships can be built and that continuity is preserved. The advantage of the former is that more people may be exposed to the issues that are explored.

• Keep your group to a size that will allow everyone to participate. (Unless you have mostly talkers or mostly listeners, 6 to 10 is usually a good number.)

• Decide whether you will include prayer, and if so, assign responsibility for structuring and leading prayer ahead of time.

• Decide whether you plan to have the study lead you to a ministry of some kind, as a group or as individuals.

• Decide whether you want to "study aging," or to explore the implications of aging for your own lives. The latter may be more threatening to some people, but allows for great personal growth to occur.

• Note whether members share some common experience or interest that might provide a focus for the group, such as having been caregivers, working on a pastoral care committee for the congregation, having an interest in developing intergenerational activities, facing retirement, or being already retired.

Aging: A Spiritual Journey

T. Herbert O'Driscoll

If we are honest, all writing about aging is autobiographical, for
either we are already aware of our aging or we anticipate it with as infinite a variety of responses as we bring to anything else. In recent
decades the succession of our years has become the stuff of much
thought, investigation, questioning, and statistical study. The reasons are
obvious. We are living longer, a statement only slightly shadowed by the
"we" being an actuarial calculation rather than a personal guarantee.
Inexorably, the mean age of our society is moving higher and higher.
The practical consequences of this trend may be readily seen.   The
more subtle effects, such as newly emerging leisure patterns, changes
in pace, tone, and priorities of thinking, will become evident more
gradually.   There will be marked effects on art, literature, and all other
products of human imagination. If wisdom really is a gift of old age, we
are perhaps bound for a more philosophical civilization. A darker
thought is the possibility that passivity, another companion of advancing years, will pervade society at levels both physical and mental.

While we can learn much from projections and statistics and calcula-
tions, we are still humbled in our efforts to foresee the quality and texture of a future in which the human life span will be significantly
lengthened. We Westerners are patently gifted in matters of technology and the production of material goods. Our capacities for enriching
the human experience and steering a safe course on the inner journey
are less certain. It is to considerations relating to the *quality* of one's
advancing years, then, that this book is oriented. It is not merely one
more book in the mounting tide of books about aging. It specifically
stakes out a territory within that process, the territory we have called
spirituality.

The moment I see that last sentence I realize how very much of the twentieth century and of Western civilization it is. It makes two assumptions that seem self-evident to us, but would be incomprehensible to earlier ages. One assumption is that human experience is sectional and that one such section is a "thing" called spirituality. The other is the assumption that there is something more inclusive or universal of which spirituality is only a part. What aspect of human experience is outside the province of the spiritual? Are there actually elements in human experience not spiritual? We have only to ask the questions to realize how much the Christian in us clashes with the acculturated twentieth-century citizen.

The answer to all such questions is, for a Christian, a resounding "No!" Human experience is unthinkable without its also being a spiritual experience from birth to death and beyond. In the life of any particular individual there may be no institutional form of spirituality, no church envelopes on the writing desk, no familiar hymns learned or creedal statements formed. But we are as much spiritual beings as we are sexual beings. To be human is to be spiritual.

The moment in the second chapter of Genesis (and it matters not at what level of the literal or the mythic we read it) when the Creator takes dust and breathes into it the breath of that same ultimate life which streams through the galaxies is the moment of our conception as spiritual beings. Far from being merely a part of our humanity, spirituality defines our humanity.

I shall age in the company of many spirits, welcome and unwelcome. Now halfway through my sixth decade, I sometimes detect the cloying presence of a spirit of self-pity, sometimes a spirit of fear, frequently a spirit of anxiety. All can at this stage be repulsed by activity, involvement, creativity, but I am under no illusion that these diversions will forever be available as allies against the invasion of those dark shadows of my being. Which spirit will be the richest and closest companion of my senior years? I do not yet know. I know what my hope is: that I may encounter one who offers new creation in exchange for my diminishing powers, bright visions for my failing sight, and intimations of resurrection for my expectations of death.

You will have noticed that I have moved from the general to the particular, from the plural to the personal. I do so for a reason. I observe that many who write about the things of our human aging adopt an objective stance. I am quite sure that frequently it is an unconscious protection against associating the self with the subject of aging. We have endless devices for this sort of thing. We reflect philosophically about aging by reaching through time and culture for jewels of wisdom dropped by the great. We offer data about an exterior and abstract thing called "aging," statistics involving white-haired legions who march in some comfortably distant decade. We use distancing language, words such as "they" and "the aged." It is said that Damien, priest on Molokai, truly became a minister to his leprous congregation the day he began his sermon to them with the words, "We lepers . . . ." We need not address our aging as a terrible disease (though much in our culture does just that), but as an aspect of human experience that will best be reflected upon by men and women who do not seek to deny its reality for themselves.

Allow, then, some personal reflection. I shall be 56 years old by the time these thoughts see print. From the vantage point of someone 20 or 25 years older, that age may be regarded as inadequate for the purposes of this book! But I am aware of certain realities. Whatever my state of health, there are changes taking place in my body, changes in appearance, in energy levels, in appetites. I am aware that within a decade I must arrive at what is still official retirement age. Within the last month I have received news of the deaths of two of my university contemporaries. I am aware, too, of other changes. Because they are taking place in my inmost being, they are more difficult to express. But the fact is that the patterns of my spirituality are changing.

I am a child of the church from birth. Growing up in the south of Ireland in the 1930s meant that I grew up in a world where Christian faith was utterly universal, where the sacredness of the natural world and the reality of the spiritual world were strongly present. Neither Enlightenment nor Industrial Revolution had yet demolished the sacred ladder set up between earth and heaven. I can recall no moment of "becoming a Christian." Flashes of awareness of the presence of God, of "epiphany," of "annunciation," have come often. In such moments, faith is realized and nourished. God comes near, Christ encounters us, our searching soul glimpses a Shining City. But like all visions, these moments are given and taken, they are found and lost and must daily be sought again, for those are the terms of our earthly relationship with the Kingdom of Heaven that surrounds us.

This process I find becoming richer in recent years. There are hints appearing in things I write, clues in my homilies and meditations. I say they are "appearing." Why do I write of it in this way? Because it is not a change I have intentionally sought. I have encountered a reality beyond myself, an "other" meeting me on my journey, a reality that first came toward me from beyond, but now walks with me and indeed has entered more and more into my being.

What is this "it"? I know, yet I shall never fully know. It is that mystery that touched me in my baptism, while I was still all unknowing of it. It has engaged my attention a thousand times in the years between, greeting my partial vision in unnumbered disguises: in the beauty of nature, in dreams, in the ecstasy of love, in the subtlety of relationships, in sacrament, in the warmth of community, in moments of solitude, in the instant of creativity.

I know that this "it" is more than an "it"; for, mystery though it be, it invades my personhood and therefore must itself be personal, must have being and identity and name. I speak, as you well know, of the Holy Spirit.

I cannot remember a time when there was not in some sense a realization of this presence, yet I am aware of it more richly in recent years. I am aware, too, of a wish to be more intentional about the exercise of this sense of presence. I have felt grateful for the moments given, for the glimpse of doorways opening on hidden levels of being. Yet I realize now that I have been a receiver rather than a discoverer. Now I wish to seek out this presence, rather than presume there will always be unexpected encounters. I find that in my reading there is less searching for more information or practical insights for ministry or parish administration. Rather, I want to explore the vast and lovely country of rich spirituality that bears the footprints and echoes with the voices of those who have experienced both the presence and absence of God as they lived out the journey I myself must pursue.

My generation has undergone many changes in its understanding of the Christian faith. The years immediately following World War II saw a "boom" in church life and organization. In a twilight decade of consensus about national objectives and social mores, the institutions of church and society in the 1950s and early 1960s saw themselves as working together for worthwhile, if rarely defined, ends.

Then came a revolution that changed and is still changing every facet of our lives. A severe questioning of all traditional values took place. Old loyalties were no longer taken for granted. Many left organized religion to follow their own quest in their own way. Hungry for spiritual food and drink, many in the 1970s turned to the East for nourishment. Many traditional practices such as yoga, genuine and therapeutic in themselves, flowed into Western life. Eastern spiritual leadership was sought and followed.

While reasons for this attraction varied, the nearest thing to a common factor was a rejection of Western activism and a longing for elements felt to be absent from the Christian tradition, at least from the Christianity of recent centuries. Among these elements were meditation, contemplation, and a sense of intimate relationship with the earth.

All this has not made recent Christian experience either comfortable or easy. Within the Christian community itself vast and deep change has had to be experienced. Sensibilities have sometimes been grievously hurt. Many have known great agony of mind and spirit. But out of this cauldron of intergenerational experience has come a new church and a new spirituality. Perhaps we should say there has come a newly vitalized church and spirituality, for much that is central to the life of faith today is ancient treasure rediscovered.

Christians of all ages are discovering the flow of energy that comes from a faith stance that is consciously chosen rather than merely inherited and therefore sometimes taken for granted. They are coming to a deeper appreciation of the sacred meal of the Christian community that we call Eucharist. They are realizing the powerful way in which it can gather a people as they journey through a wilderness of change and threat. They are realizing that however fine and dignified our formal religion may have been, there may also have been an aspect of shallowness. There is in many a sense of moving into something deeper and richer. External things, things learned cerebrally, are yielding their single dominance to include more richly the internal, the experienced, the intuited. We are recovering a sense of mind and heart informing us equally. Christian religion has rediscovered Christian spirituality. Religious system is enriched by spiritual journey. Faith is being more and more understood not merely as a body of knowledge we do or do not believe but also as a mystery which can give meaning to our experience and become a resource for our daily living.

At the heart of all this, a revitalized liturgy proclaims the central and indispensable truth for this or for any other generation of Christians.

> *Christ has died.*
> *Christ is risen.*
> *Christ will come again.*

That short exclamation sings that human life is not merely a journeying away from a youthful innocent awareness of Christ as Lord and friend toward a sad and wiser adulthood beyond such naivete. We possess a Christ who is the resource for this hour and for all that lies ahead. He is Lord of the past, the present, and the future. Our years are a life-long pilgrimage toward him.

Much more follows from that realization. The central events of Christian faith take place not only in the past but within the ongoing experience of our daily lives. Bethlehem and Calvary and the Garden Tomb are not merely places in a long-ago time or a faraway geography. Daily within each of us something of God seeks to come to birth. Each of us is potentially a Bethlehem. When I wrong or betray or hurt others, there is a sense in which I crucify them. In like fashion, I am myself subjected to little crucifixions. In such ways each of us can become a Calvary. But then the mystery we know as resurrection can also take place within each of us. We can recover from crushing defeat. We can transform destructive attitudes. Faith can overcome doubt, despair give way to joy. In such experiences we possess in ourselves the transforming power of resurrection.

Within the last 10 years Christian faith has shown an immensely creative response to the spiritual hunger felt by a whole searching Western culture. We have realized the extent to which Western culture, affected by such events as the Enlightenment and the Industrial Revolution, allowed the meditative and contemplative experience, as well as the creation-centered aspects of Christian tradition, to be nearly forgotten by all but a few. Timeless Christian spiritualities are again nourishing us, particularly the Celtic, Franciscan, and Orthodox. Also available to us, yet for the most part spurned and misunderstood, are the deep insights of Native American spirituality, such as those of Chief Seattle. We are seeing more and more accessible translations of writings from all of these sources. We are hearing the voices that have spoken to us of such things in our own time, voices such as those of

Teilhard de Chardin, E. F. Schumacher, Donald Allchin, Alan Ecclestone, Urban Holmes, and Madeleine L'Engle. All offer themselves to us as we seek spiritual resources for the future.

One other element of contemporary spirituality must be named. For a long time the Christian message was focused on personal life, its relevance seen primarily in terms of the individual. Still, there have always been those who challenged such a limited vision. Old Testament prophets inveighed against it in their day, John Wesley and Elizabeth Fry in theirs. We have heard Dorothy Day, Thomas Merton, Martin Luther King Jr., Dietrich Bonhoeffer. These men and women, and many others, would claim that Christ is Lord not only of personal life, but also Lord and Judge of institutions—corporate, political, and, for that matter, ecclesiastical.

While many of our generation have found it difficult to understand this aspect of Christian spirituality, it has helped to create links between our faith and our daily participation in corporate and political structures. We are coming to see that we follow one who is Lord of all aspects of our experience.

I am convinced that those of us who will live out our senior years through the close of this century are the fortunate recipients of a rich inheritance of spirituality only recently recovered. To realize this can be a most valuable corrective when we are in a mood to lament the quality of our time in history and to cry with Hamlet,

> *The time is out of joint; O cursed spite,*
> *That ever I was born to set it right!*

You and I have seen much storm and noise of battle. We have seen our most deeply held beliefs and traditions brutally challenged. We have heard faith questioned, moral positions attacked, God dismissed as dead. To all this, you and I have been far more than spectators. By our decisions, our ideas, our energy, you and I, wittingly or not, have contributed to the totality of what is now afoot. And the world has been transformed before our eyes into a place of vast complexity, immense achievement, unprecedented danger.

In the contemporary wilderness there may be bitter waters, but there are also the sweetest and purest of deep-flowing wells. There may be hunger in our weary twentieth-century souls, but there is a spiritual bread that is fulfilling, energizing, and inexhaustible. We are pilgrims well supplied for the journey, supplied by the Lord of the city to which we go.

Deo gratias!

Study Guide

Aging: A Spiritual Journey

Reflection Questions

- Draw a time line on a sheet of paper, dividing it into the decades of your life. Above the line, jot a brief note in each decade that describes how you remember your relationship with God at that age. Below the line, jot a brief note about how you remember your view of yourself in each decade. How has your understanding of yourself and God changed over the years?

- Most of the media portray aging in powerfully negative terms. Is the idea that aging can be a spiritual journey a viable alternative? How have you experienced aging as a spiritual journey? What landmarks have been significant?

- O'Driscoll states that all human experience is spiritual and that "faith is . . . a mystery which can give meaning to our experience and become a resource for our daily living." In what ways can you claim this to be true in the lives of others who have influenced your faith journey? In your own life?

- "I shall age in the company of many spirits, welcome and unwelcome," says the author. Which spirits have been most welcome and most unwelcome to you? Which spirits do you hope will be "the richest and closest companion(s) of (your) senior years?"

- "I cannot remember a time when there was not in some sense a realization of this presence (the Holy Spirit), yet I am aware of it more richly in recent years. I am aware, too, of a wish to be more intentional about the exercise of this sense of presence. . . . Now I wish to seek out this presence, rather than presume there will always be unexpected encounters." How have you/do you/could you "seek out" the presence of the Holy Spirit in your life?

- ". . . Christ is Lord not only of personal life, but also Lord and Judge of institutions—corporate, political, and, for that matter, ecclesiastical. . .

. And the world has been transformed before our eyes into a place of vast complexity, immense achievement, unprecedented danger." Where do you see and experience Christ's presence in that world? How do you see God calling us to live in the midst of that world? How has your perspective on this changed over the years?

• O'Driscoll comments on the stresses and the gifts of our time. "There may be hunger in our weary, twentieth-century souls, but there is a spiritual bread that is fulfilling, energizing, and inexhaustible." It has been said that our hunger is planted in us by God, calling us to God's Self. Where do you find yourself hungry? What feeds you? How can you feed others or help them to find food?

Group Process

Purpose: To enable participants to assess the place of spirituality in their own life journeys.

Step 1:   Divide into small groups. A minimum of four groups is necessary. Assign each group one of the following statements or questions. Using the book, they are to list ways the author understands spirituality as it relates to the assigned statement.

1.   How has "it" been known to the author?

2.   What changes in society and the church have affected present spirituality?

3.   Our faith story is more than past event—it is also present reality.

4.   Christ is not just a personal Savior, but Lord and Judge of institutions.

Step 2:   Reconvene and invite each group to share its findings.

Step 3:   Give the group members an opportunity to reflect silently. Some may want to jot down their throughts on the following questions. What responses from your own spiritual life can you make to the four statements? What aspects of your life in the Christian community have been helpful?

Step 4:   Divide the group into pairs of younger and older partners to share Step 3 insights. Ask them to look for similarities and differences. Is age a factor? Why? Why not?

Step 5:   Reconvene and allow time for sharing any general observations and feelings and/or learnings about the chapter.

Ethics and the Third Age

Charles J. Fahey

Ethics and the Spiritual Life

At the outset of this essay it is important to establish the relationship between ethics and holiness, reflection and spirituality. It is quite natural for the believer who, with God's grace, struggles to know the Lord's will and, to do it and thus achieve holiness, to consign ethics to the realm of the practical philosopher and in turn, for the philosopher and, to assign the quest for holiness to the theologian and the individual believer. Nothing could be further from the truth. Ethics is the science and art of doing the right thing in the light of human reason. Holiness for the believer is trying to do the right thing in the light of Christ's message.

While the word *spirituality* immediately evokes the image of life animated by faith for the believer, it can mean a reflective life without reference to any transcendence for others.

This essay is written from the perspective that the believer and nonbeliever are pressed to deal with new realities of the end of the twentieth century. These realities involve issues laden with values and involve not only our personal, interior lives but also the social life of the whole community.

It is built on the premise that the riddles and paradoxes of a prolonged life span can be approached adequately only by reason informed by faith and that good ethics and sound spirituality are inseparable.

The Third Age: A New Reality

Although society is not fully aware of it, the latter part of the twentieth century has seen the evolution of a new part of the life cycle: the third age. It is that period of life which follows the ordinary period of parenting and that time in which most persons would normally be at the highest level of productivity. While humankind has always had older people in its midst, they have been an exception rather than the rule.

Our capacity to reflect, to develop clear and distinct ideas, to experiment and to apply our ever-new understandings to life has resulted in various techniques and strategies that help us to ward off predators, natural and human, which would bring an early death. Interventions throughout the various parts of the life course have decreased mortality at every stage of life. This has resulted in the third age becoming expected or, in a technical sense, normal; surely a triumph of the human spirit.

Not only do more persons survive into the third age, but most contemporary elders also experience lives that are not only longer but are less painful and uncertain, are filled with more leisure and opportunities for cultural, educational, recreational, and interpersonal relationships than at any other moment of history.

Even as we are in the midst of demographic revolution with the dramatic growth of even the "old old," we are in an epidemiological revolution as well. In another age, persons died rather quickly from parasitic and infectious diseases. As we have developed improved public health measures and early interventions such as immunization, we are moving toward death by reason of chronic, degenerative diseases, many of which are associated with the aging process.

The third age is an uncharted period of life. Today's elders are "writing the book," developing cultural patterns and social structures not only for themselves and future generations of older persons but also for society as a whole.

All development is ambiguous. Our ability to develop new things seems to outstrip our capacity to develop values and structures concerning their use. Atomic power, pesticides, and even ventilators, are all good in themselves, but they have the potential to compromise human dignity and, perhaps, destroy us as well.

The third age is a triumph of science. However, it could cause much pain and even contribute to the demise of our species. Thus the third age brings with it an ethical agenda for individuals and society as a whole.

In the scheme of creation humans share a great deal with other living things, particularly animals. In God's providence the ordinary life course is closely related to the needs of the species for survival. In each species the life span is sufficiently long for reproduction and the continuation of the species. The normal life cycle is twofold: from gestation to sexual maturity and from reproduction through parenting and then death. We humans have upset this natural development. We have developed the third age, a period of life that is needed neither for reproduction nor, in a narrow sense, for production.

The most fundamental ethical issue facing us is the meaning of the third age for the species, for society and the individual.

The Necessity of Discernment

Holiness and good ethics both involve discernment and behavior. The individual believer must constantly assess his or her life in its social context and in the light of the gospel message. In a broader sense the church must read the signs of the times, integrating insights from the various sciences with the precious treasury of scripture and tradition. This corporate discernment process is necessary if the gospel is to make sense to contemporary humankind. Furthermore, the power of faith will help the broader society and individuals develop approaches to make the third age a fruitful and satisfying period.

Whether the third age is a blessing or a curse, permanent or a blip in the evolutionary processes, is still a matter of conjecture. It seems the answer lies in the way we humans will order our personal lives and social relations.

Social and Personal Ethics

Ethical issues generated by the third age involve two distinct but interrelated areas of inquiry, the social and the personal. Social ethics involve questions of societal structures and their efficacy in assisting individuals to realize their life plans and to live in harmony with one another. Personal ethics are concerned with the way individuals live with themselves and in society. The church has a role of discernment and teaching in both areas. Individual holiness is to be found not only in faith and baptism, but also in living the gospel individually (personal ethics) and in contributing to a kingdom of justice and peace (social ethics).

Social Ethics

The third age challenges all basic social institutions; the family, the economy, the workplace, health care delivery, and political life. It exacerbates population pressures and all the ethical issues inherent therein.

Inevitably, the development of the third age is a source of intergenerational tension. It is not a question of whether it will exist, but rather how well will society manage it. In turn, leadership in the quest for harmony falls squarely on the shoulders of those in the third age.

Four living generations are now more usual than not, and five are becoming more common. People who remain married will spend more time without children in the home than with them. What is it to be a husband and wife in the third age? How does the scriptural admonition to honor your father and mother play itself out at a time when there are two generations in the third age?

Divorce and remarriage are realities in contemporary society. A sociogram of many American families is very complex, posing real questions about the relationships within and among the generations.

We live in a period in which we do not need the number of people to produce the goods, if not the services, society has needed in the past. Economists and political leaders alike are concerned about structural changes in the economy. They agree that economic growth in the developed countries cannot be sustained without significant growth in the economies of the less-developed countries of the world; countries poor in technology and capital and with a labor force that is burgeoning but relatively unskilled.

An economic summit of the Group of Seven held in Detroit in March 1994 focused on the alarming rates of unemployment in most of the member countries. Leaders of the United States delegation took little solace in the fact that their country had generated more jobs than any other (some 38 million in recent years), because so many were relatively unskilled and low paying. For the first time, some economists wondered whether increased productivity would mean the creation of new jobs for displaced workers.

What does this have to with the third age? The answer is at once simple and daunting. The economic well-being of most older persons is dependent on their continued connectedness with production, either directly through employment or indirectly by participation in pensions and Social Security.

While Social Security and pensions have been developed to afford older persons a degree of dignity and security in retirement, at least part of the rationale has been to encourage older workers to leave the work force and give younger persons an opportunity to fill their roles.

Both Social Security and pensions are dependent upon the productivity of the current work force and its willingness to support the retired. The continued viability of both structures rests upon the delicate moral and political balancing of the interests of both the employed and the retired.

The elderly's access to basic health care poses similar issues. In 1965 Medicare and Medicaid were enacted into law to assure health care for the needy and the elderly. Millions of persons, both old and young, have benefited from these programs. However, each is supported by those currently working, some of whom have no insurance.

Continued support of these or similar programs is likely to continue only if we have a national program to assure access to service for all without undue burden on any individuals. The distribution of burdens and benefits in society is everyone's concern. Persons of all ages must be involved in building structures that will serve people in changing times. Older persons have an especially important moral role to play.

It should be clear that the voice of the elderly in the development of just, sound social structures is a matter not only of justice but also of enlightened self-interest; yet it remains unclear whether their considerable political clout will focus only on issues of concern to them, or on the needs of all of society and generations yet unborn.

Personal Ethics

Inertia, distraction, and denial are the psychological and spiritual enemies of the third age. The morally and spiritually vital life is the examined life.

Unfortunately, while our social circumstances change and our physiological being changes as well, we tend to ignore both.

The ethically and spiritually alive person is aware and sensitive. That person is given to determine, when possible, what course of action is preferable, and when beyond one's control how one will react to it. Such people recognize options and alternatives as well as limitations and barriers. It is sound, both psychologically and spiritually, in the construct of the distinguished scholar Paul Baltys, to "select, optimize and compensate" all through life but particularly in the third age. This is in marked contrast to an unexamined and drifting life that is far too often the experience of older persons.

Thus, the first and foremost ethical challenge is whether to decide or not to decide, to make choices or to let inertia prevail.

For many, time and relief from the responsibilities entailed in employment and family life are among the gifts of the third age. For some, these gifts can mean loneliness and boredom; for others, opportunities to be engaged, hospitable, and to grow in wisdom. For some, this is an opportunity only for a self-centeredness and withdrawal; for others, growth in both the interior life and in interactions with others. It can mean a time of ministry to others now that the preoccupations with family and work are no longer at the center of attention.

Sickness, dependency, and death can occur at any point in life, but they are ever more pressing realities as one passes through the third age. Contemporary culture tends to deny these realities, yet this is foreign to the asceticism associated with Christianity. While not seeking these things in and of themselves, they are a time of grace for those enduring them and those who serve.

Perhaps more dreaded than death itself is the process of dying. In a series of books and lectures Daniel Callahan (for example, *The Troubled*

Dream of Life, Living with Mortality) has called modern medicine to task for unduly distorting the dying process. In his judgment, both in basic science and in clinical practice, medicine seems to be pursuing the siren call of a natural immortality.

Each of us must deal with our personal frailty and mortality even as we participate in a variety of venues about appropriate attitudes and public policies.

The Church and the Third Age

The church has multiple roles to play as it assists individuals and society with this new reality.

We need rituals, modern sacraments if you will, to help persons as they enter the third age. These events could help people to understand how they have lived their lives and how they might use their gifts in the future. They could assure the support of the believing community as persons enter fully and enthusiastically into the third age, with all of its uncertainties and opportunities.

The church should be present to help people each step of the way to grow old gracefully.

It must help persons understand and accept their call to ministry and their call to be ministered to.

It should make sure that the frail, the sick, the dependent among us feel the healing power of Christ, particularly as it is evidenced by a caring Christian community.

The church should be in dialogue with the broader society and help it develop public policy that is just for all people. It should contribute to the creation of structures that are stable, predictable, and sustainable.

The church should be part of the evolution of a cultural vision of growing old and being old that can help sustain individuals and serve as basis for sound relationships within and among the generations. This vision should be based in realities of the aging process, be in accord with human dignity, evoke a notion of social significance through which older persons can contribute to the continuation of the human species and contribute to stewardship of the environment in which we live.

The providential gift of the third age brings with it awesome personal and social responsibilities.

Study Guide

Ethics and the Third Age

Reflection Questions

• What is your understanding of or definition of "ethics" and "holiness"? Write it down; then look at Fahey's definitions at the beginning of his article. Compare and contrast your understanding with his.

• Fahey says that "holiness and good ethics involve both discernment and behavior" and that the discernment process is corporate. What corporate processes do you participate in that help you discern what is right and help you decide what to do? What corporate processes exist in our society? In our congregations? How might we establish such corporate processes? Why is it important that discernment be done corporately rather than individually? In what situations might it be important to act corporately rather than individually?

• Fahey says that a balanced distribution of burdens and benefits in society is everyone's concern. What was the balance of burdens and benefits between the generations 50 years ago? 25 years ago? What is it now? What might it be in the next 25 years? What will happen to that balance when the baby-boomers (born 1946 to 1964), who compose one-third of the U.S. population, enter the third age followed by much smaller populations? How will balance be maintained? What changes in society might we face? How do we decide what is ethical in light of the needs of different generations?

• "Thus, the first and foremost ethical challenge is whether to decide or not to decide, to make choices or to let inertia prevail." Think about "third-agers" you know who "decide" and who do not "decide." What is the difference in their lives? If you are a third-ager, to what extent do you feel you make choices versus letting inertia prevail? How do you feel about the difference between choosing or letting external forces chose for you? If you are not a third-ager, what would you like to do when you reach that age, and how do you think it will affect your life?

• What does your congregation do to help third-agers (and others) discern and chose behaviors that are ethical and holy? What could your congregation do that would help you in this area?

Group Process

Step 1:   Post a sheet of newsprint on which you have written the quotes: "Ethics is the science . . . of doing the right thing in light of human reason." "Holiness for the believer is trying to do the right thing in light of Christ's message." Ask the group to identify situations in which they think people of goodwill could disagree depending on which of the two statements is their primary operative statement. In other words, when might a person who is not a Christian come to one conclusion based on reason, when a Christian might come to another conclusion based on the gospel? Do not discuss each situation, merely list it in a few words. After five or six situations have been listed, ask the group to select one to discuss. (If there are more than 16 people in the group, select an additional situation to discuss).

Step 2:   Divide the group into two teams with 4 to 8 members on each team. Give Team 1 the statement: "Ethics is the science of doing the right thing in light of human reason." Give Team 2 the statement: "Holiness for the believer is trying to do the right thing in light of Christ's message." Using the situation identified in Step 1, ask each team to take ten minutes to prepare what they will say to the other team to articulate their stand. (If there are more than 16 people in the group, use the second situation identified in Step 1 and create two additional teams to address that situation; give these two teams the same quotes.)

Step 3:   Reconvene the larger group and ask the two teams to discuss their situation for ten minutes. If there are two situations (and four teams) limit the discussion time to 5 to 7 minutes for each situation.

Step 4:   Reconvene the larger group. Ask how a Christian might go about discerning what to do in each situation. At some point, remind participants of the triad "scripture, tradition, and reason" identified in Fahey's article. Also encourage the group to consider Fahey's position that such discernment must be communal. How does your congregation help people with such decisions? How could your congregation help?

Step 5:   Fahey says that a balanced distribution of burdens and benefits in society is everyone's concern. In the larger group (if less than 20) or in smaller groups discuss: What was the balance of burdens and benefits between the generations 50 years ago? 25 years ago? What is it now? What might it be in the next 25 years? What will happen to that balance when the baby-boomers (born 1946 to 1964), who compose one-third of the U.S. population, enter the third age followed by much smaller populations. How will balance be maintained? What changes in society might we face? How do we decide what is ethical in light of the needs of different generations?

Step 6:   Invite participants to reflect silently and write the burdens and benefits they anticipate for themselves and how they hope/want those burdens and benefits to be balanced with other generations. After 5 minutes, ask each person to find a partner and take 5 to 7 minutes to share what they chose from their list and/or what they have learned today.

Step 7:   Reconvene the larger group and invite participants to say what they have learned or would like to say to the larger group.

Challenge to Ministry:
Opportunities for Older Persons

Emma Lou Benignus

These thoughts concerning older adults, their roles and responsible participation in society, are addressed to the churches. Therefore, we turn to our Jewish-Christian heritage for an understanding of the possible, rather than only to secular data and theories of aging. Let the reader be warned: We shall explore the questions that arise with a bias we proudly own.

It is to be hoped that in the next decades the church's concept of ministry of the laos (the whole people of God) will:

- Recognize that the most elderly, as well as the young, are potential channels of God's grace;

- Realize that spiritual gifts and the fruit of the Spirit are given by the Holy Spirit to old people, too, for their fulfillment and for their use in ministry;

- Be supportive of old people's yearnings to relate and to contribute;

- Be aware that a person can be born anew at any age.

When asked what they wish, rather than what they need, many older persons say, "To make a contribution," "To let the remaining years count," and even "To help my family by dying well." A woman of 85 who had just heard a prognosis of her imminent death turned from her doctor to her priest to say, "Being dead and gone doesn't bother me, but what I do want is to make it clear to people that life lived here with God is every bit worth living all the way through. I don't want to contradict that in any way. If I begin to garble that message, will you help me keep it straight?"

Note that this old woman:

- Realizes her way of living and dying can convey a message about God;

- Is quite clear about the statement she wants her life to make, that with God life is good;

- Knows she might, in spite of her intentions, betray the best she knows;

- Looks to her fellow Christian to help keep her faithful.

To have a mission, a purpose, a contribution to make and "promises to keep," and to want to come through to the last of one's days with integrity are the activity of the Spirit within. The physical limitations of aging may actually enhance this inner life. "Physical decline may limit productivity, but the activity of the Spirit continues through shifting the central focus of personal identity from doing-in-the-world to being-in-the-world, from what one does to who one is. As physical activity diminishes, the movement of the Spirit is toward an emphasis upon the nonphysical aspects of life. We all know individuals who in the face of seemingly overwhelming physical disintegration still face life with vitality that clearly is not based in their physical well-being. This vitality is evidence of their Spirit at work. It is plainly recognizable in the later years of life."[1]

To fail to engage this Spirit or carelessly to deny a person's capacity to serve is to consign that individual to loneliness and close down a life before its natural time. The experience of an aged man comes to mind. Early one morning he was found peeling potatoes and humming to himself in the kitchen of the "home" in which he lived. Curtly reprimanded for his intrusion and punished by being confined to his room for the rest of the day, he muttered, "A man's got to be a man to live." Here it was: the yen to "be up and at it," the desire to do something of value, the longing to take part in life as others do. Do we nurture these values in childhood only to quell them in old age? We need to understand that, deprived of significant living, many die spiritually before their physical death.

We know a 98-year-old, tormented by an unpredictable heart and limited sight, who struggles daily to transcend her situation. She longs to walk outdoors, visiting the places in the garden and woods of the nursing home that have become dear to her, to feel the sunlight and wind on her body. But for safety's sake she has been forbidden to leave the porch unless someone walks with her. That someone seldom comes. On a particularly fresh day, as she leaned sadly against the porch screen, memory carried her back to a childhood visit to the zoo. She felt again the distress of seeing a chimpanzee confined to its cage when it so clearly wanted out, to do what monkeys do, to swing in the trees of the monkey yard as the others were. Now their lives were painfully alike, that chimp's and hers.

She returned to the living room, where a cheery soul said, "It's lovely out in the yard today, isn't it, Helen?" To her surprise she heard herself say, "Don't bother to call me Helen, just call me Chimp." With a laugh, and a tear on her cheek, she went to her room. What did she do there? With tears flowing copiously now, she beseeched God to care for the innocent animals of this world—all those destroyed by our pollution and greed in the arrogant conviction that they belong to us rather than to their Creator. Then she sent a check to a young grandnephew, asking him to plant a tree in some spot where children might play in its shade and birds build their nests in its branches.

This kind of loving interplay with all that is, is one of the Spirit's gifts to older people. Out of their own pain and longing comes a heightened sensitivity to the needs of others. When society diminishes these persons' self-esteem by viewing them only as recipients with nothing to contribute, it takes away hope and meaning. We might ascribe such error to social ignorance of human nature. But when the church of Jesus Christ persistently supports only ministry *to* rather than also ministry *by* the elderly, it compounds society's sin.

The year 1935 marked the beginning of Social Security and the arbitrary designation of 65 as the age for mandatory retirement. It was expected that retirement with a modicum of assured income would give opportunity for the freedom to pursue one's choices. It was not expected that retirement would carry social opprobrium, or the message, "You're through now, someone else is replacing you. Forget all this and have a good time . . . somewhere else." Many negatives were suddenly linked with the 65th year. American society, including the churches, has on the whole accepted this negation of human resourcefulness with dehumanizing indifference.

But now the rapid increase in the number of people over 65 who enjoy good health and are mentally alert is turning apathy into protest. "Retire at 65 to sit around for 30 years? Not I!" Initiatives that express the emancipation of the elderly are having an impact. Magazines feature articles on America's "lively generation," people in their "spectacular 80s" who "celebrate the silver."[2] There are many among us, such as Bob Hope, Katherine Hepburn, and George Burns, who are cultivating their talents, continuing their careers or launching into new ones, identifying capacities they never knew they had and going back to school for the joy of learning. The stereotypes and myths are being put to rout. We are beginning to recognize that 65 can launch a time of precious freedom to become reacquainted with ourselves, to follow the leading of the heart, the leading of the Spirit, and once again to play. Our younger years, with their heavy stress on success, status, making money, acquiring a home and family, tended to be shaped by external prescriptions and peer-conditioned values. We often found ourselves involved in decisions we would have preferred not to make, participating in programs and enterprises we could not personally endorse. But now, at retirement age, we approach a freedom heretofore unclaimed.

It is unfortunate when the local church does nothing at the time of a parishioner's retirement to remind him or her that every member of the body of Christ is drawn into the company of the Spirit, the church, and that every member therein is endowed with charisms, gifts of grace, and significant spiritual capacities to be used for the good of all.[3] "To each is given the manifestation of the Spirit for the common good" (1 Cor. 12:7).

The church's role is to awaken each of us to our giftedness. With Paul, it must say, "I remind you to rekindle the gift of God that is within you" (2 Tim. 1:6). Discern how God has been present in your life all these years. How does God call you now to be friend and servant, relating with Jesus Christ to the world God loves? The privileged role of Christian friends in the congregation is to support the retiree, to recognize that "God did not give us a spirit of cowardice, but a spirit of power and love and self-discipline" (2 Tim. 1:7). In such circumstances, with fellow Christians we can find the courage to take on our share of both joy and suffering for the sake of the gospel of God who "called us with a holy calling, not according to our works but according to his own purpose and grace. This grace was given to us in Christ Jesus before the ages began" (2 Tim. 1:9).

With such reminders stirring them to action, a group of older church women became active in the Civil Rights movement in the 1960s. They gathered momentum and supporters as they moved through the communities. Their dignity and informed declarations on behalf of civil rights and justice for all citizens gave others the courage to speak out too. Several found themselves in jail, two of them wives of retired bishops and one the mother of a state governor. In a newspaper interview they expressed the wonder they found in being older and being free to witness to the values and conditions they hoped would prevail throughout the country, not only for the sake of the deprived but also for the sake of their own grandchildren and their children, that all might be free to become the persons God endows them to be.

These women gave classic expression through their civil rights ministry to the mark of maturity identified by psychologist Erik Erikson in his well-known account of human development, *Childhood and Society*. As people move through their years, they come into different stages of concern and openness. The psychologically more mature tend to develop concern for the welfare of oncoming generations, as opposed to a primary fascination with their own good. Erikson's term for this capacity is "generativity," the gift of caring about the good of those yet to come. Another capacity that marks maturity as reported by Erikson is the desire for personal integrity, for life to be authentic, for coherence between professed values and life as actually lived. This yearning comes through in common parlance as a desire to set the record straight, to be accountable for one's life. When passions such as these dominate our later years, it is not surprising that the heart and conscience of many older people are opened afresh to the Christian gospel. Wellsprings of love and commitment deeper than ever before can be known in these years. These late-life gifts are meant to be used.

As one reads the Hebrew and Christian Testaments, it is easy to gain the impression that when God wanted to bring about a significant change in the world, old people were called to the fore. Abraham and Sarah, both in their 90s, were the channels through whom God began a lineage of Israelites. When Israel was captive in Egypt, Moses, his brother Aaron, and his sister Miriam, already in their 60s, were summoned to lead and console the people in their 40 years of wandering in the desert. When something utterly new was about to break upon the world, the elderly Elizabeth and Zechariah were entrusted with the birth and rearing of John who became the Baptist, herald of his cousin Jesus.

The older man Joseph was given to Mary as husband, ostensibly to protect her in a situation too daunting for youth. After the angel's annunciation to young Mary, she "went in haste" to spend three months with Elizabeth and Zechariah and was steadied in faith through the company and wisdom of this older couple. When the infant Jesus was presented in the temple, it was old Simeon, staving off death, who first recognized him as the awaited Messiah and who warned Mary that her heart would be pierced by her son's suffering (Luke 2:34-35). And then the very old prophetess Anna, long cloistered in the Temple, when she saw Jesus "gave thanks to God" and went out to speak of him to all who were looking for the redemption of Jerusalem. Not only were these older persons vehicles of divine action, but they spoke prophetically through canticles and hymns that have become part of the treasured liturgy of the Western church: Zechariah's *Benedictus* (Luke 1:78-79), Simeon's *Nunc Dimittis* (Luke 2:29-32).

John Koenig, a former professor at Union Theological Seminary, wrote in his sensitive essay *The Older Person's Worth in the Eyes of God* that in Luke's gospel

New things happen to older people. . . . [They] receive a vital ministry to perform for Israel, precisely in their last days. In fact, it is only in old age that they come to experience their true vocation. . . .

In Luke's treatment of older people we do not find the conventional expectation encountered in most cultures. . . that the aged are primarily bearers and guardians of ancient wisdom. No, according to Luke, God chooses old people as bearers and proclaimers of the New Creation. They are visionaries, futurists, people charismatically gifted with a clearer picture of God's unfolding plan than their younger brothers and sisters.[4]

Paul's New Testament letters present elderly persons as trailblazers and adventurers in God's creation. Paul himself was 60 when he planned his new and most extensive ministry in Spain (Rom. 15:22-29). Summing up his findings about old and young in scripture, John Koenig gives these comments:

The young see visions, they are intoxicated by novelty. Age helps them to distinguish between true and false novelty. . . to see the "big picture" of God's plan for salvation. . . .

In spite of losses and physical disability, degeneration is not the core of reality. For Christians, the really real is transformation, a daily re-sensitizing of ourselves to the . . . goodness of God out of which new ministries by older persons can emerge. No one is too old to experience a blossoming of charismatic gifts for ministry. No one's life is too far gone to become a place for the Spirit's empowering self-disclosure.[5]

In his 70s Senator Hubert Humphrey bore testimony to the Spirit's power. When he was free of responsibility to the administration of which he long had been a part, the senator acknowledged that his deepest intuitive insights had warned him of the folly of the Vietnam War and that he profoundly regretted not heeding the word he had heard spoken deep inside himself. The courage of this belated public confession by a revered senior statesman has itself been a continuing word of inspiration, integrity, and hope for old and young alike at this time of intense value confusion.

Senator Humphrey's story brings to mind the encounter between the incredulous elder Nicodemus and Jesus in John's Gospel (John 3:1-6). Jesus said that to "see" the kingdom of God one must be born anew (reoriented). To this Nicodemus, obviously thinking of physical birth, asked "How can anyone be born after having grown old?" Can a senior citizen be born anew? Indeed! The issue for Jesus here is nothing less than transformation, change in a person's inner life so radical as to be described as a new birth, possible at any age for those who are open to the spirit of the ever-creating God. "The wind blows where it wills," among old and young, rich and poor, strong and weak. Barclay's commentary on John's Gospel describes the effect: "It is to have something happen to the soul which can only be described as being born all over again; and the whole process is not a human achievement because it comes from the grace and power of God."[6]

Through God's great mercy it is possible in the midst of the threatening insecurities of old age to let go, to let the perishable, the transitory, however dear to us, be "washed clean away" by grace. It is possible to turn from all the illusory "saviors" one has clung to throughout life and abandon one's self in faith. The highly vulnerable later decades, with their incomparable, unpredictable, often uncontrollable experiences, are usually life's most fertile field for sensitivity to the Spirit and for sinking our roots ever more deeply into the fullest possible personal relationship with Jesus Christ. In loving him we do not stop cherishing people and situations and things dear to the heart. On the contrary, the heart expands to cherish all of creation as our Lord does. Carl Jung called the lifelong years of aging life's spiritual journey. At midlife, according to Jung, we shift from an initial acquisitive posture to one of relinquishment, voluntary or involuntary. The element of trust at this point is imperative. In trust, we can be free to reply, "Yes, Lord, let your will, not mine, be done. I will follow to the end of my days." Then, regardless of age, the Spirit will provide the capacities required and may even indulge the faithful with gifts of amazing grace.

Opportunities for ministry change with the changing times and circumstances of the older person. The cliché "Where there's a will, there's a way" is often proved valid. What God makes of our offering, however small, is God's business, as is illustrated in Mark 12:43-44. A poor widow gave two small coins, and Jesus said to his disciples, "This poor widow has put in more than all those who are contributing to the treasury. For all of them have contributed out of their abundance; but she out of her poverty has put in everything she had." As we give to others all that we have left to give—a hand wave, a smile, a look of gratitude, a word of praise—and offer it in Jesus' name, we take part in ministry. A woman on the edge of blindness, with very little left of a once-abundant life, begins her day by standing at her window, where all she sees is a bit of light, and praises God for the gift of life. "It is wonderful so to enjoy God's riches," she says. Her daily prayers of praise and the love she radiates pervade the home where she resides.

The book *I Can Still Pray*[7] speaks of the spiritual capacities of the elderly. It is a tribute to a woman whose body had been deteriorating for 21 years. Now, after yet another stroke, she was physically helpless. When a visitor began to commiserate, she countered optimistically, "But I can still pray." In circumstances of extreme limitation she found purpose for her life and reminded her visitor that she retained the most basic of functions for a God-related, faith-filled life—the capacity to pray!

Because he believed in the reality of spiritual power, a young minister wanted as much of it as possible circulating in the congregation. So he invited the six housebound members of the church to form a prayer team with him. Every week the Sunday service is taped and delivered, along with copies of the intercession list, to each team member. Although separated, the team has a corporate prayer time every morning when the priest is saying the daily office. Thereafter, throughout the week, several times each day, they offer prayers for people on the intercession list or hold them before God in meditation. The priest and team meet weekly by means of a telephone conference, and he spends an hour with each of them every six weeks to discuss their own spiritual development. Currently, one of the men on the team is helping a recent convert learn to pray. One of the women has a small prayer and Bible study group that meets regularly in her home.

When the Episcopal Church introduced *Age in Action* in the church schools, each teacher was urged to invite an older person or two to share a class session, giving young and old a chance to interact. In some churches this has become an avenue of weekly continuing intergenerational contact in a setting where the norm separates the ages for learning. In class, children and elderly can pray together and discuss that about which they pray. In imagination they can relive Bible stories, envisioning themselves as companions of Jesus, and then talk about the experience. With activities of this sort, the scriptures and the faith journey become meeting ground for the generations.

For older adults who come to church, an occasional opportunity for a leadership role is important not only for them, but for the rest of the congregation as well. A lay reader who could no longer climb steps reads the lesson from his pew with the aid of a microphone. A long-retired rector, still dear to the congregation, was invited back for homecoming Sunday. Now in a wheelchair, he preached from the center aisle. His very presence was a gift to young and old alike. Practical solutions to difficult situations can always be found if the desire is there.

A widow, desperate with pain over her husband's sudden death when they were both 70, continued to "pray a psalm a day" as they had done all their married life. But now she also read the psalm aloud to transcribe it on tape. When the tape was filled she gave it and a small recorder to a widowed blind man, all but lost in grief not unlike hers. Her reaching out to him was the beginning of his return to sociability and, later, to the church.

The losses of later life cannot be escaped, but they can be transcended to become occasions of spiritual growth as we learn to incorporate them into ministry on behalf of others. In a profound sort of way, ministry is not really an option; it is an essential expression of the nature of our being, an avenue of our fulfillment, our response to being made in the image and likeness of God.

In God's amazing way with us, when needs arise the answer is usually already there somewhere, "waiting in the bush" as was the ram when God asked Abraham to give up Isaac. There is great need today for the loving care of young children, as mounting economic pressures send more mothers to work and as single-parent families proliferate. The incidence of child abuse increases steadily. Where is the answer? In part it may lie in matching these patterns with another social phenomenon—the largest number of available grandparents and great-grandparents in good health our society has ever seen. We need each other.

Our housing patterns and industrial mobility, plus our affluence, tend to separate the generations in this country. Thus there is a great opportunity for many older men and women to lend a hand to working parents and their children as surrogate grandparents. Family Friends, a new form of three-generational ministry, has been launched by the National Council on the Aging in Washington, D.C. Volunteers are in homes one to three times a week to be with young children, or with chronically ill or disabled persons to relieve the family care-givers. Participants in this program can be reimbursed for expenses, travel, and meals, so that none who are willing need be deprived of the opportunity to give of themselves.[8]

There is more value and carryover influence than meets the eye in this kind of relationship. From a survey of professional colleagues, the author of this article discovered that when seeking inspiration and value, the memory turns to a grandparent or grandparent surrogate more frequently than to any other significant person.

The ministry of hospitality was lauded in Jesus' day. Can the senior members of our society restore it? One summer the Church of the Brethren made travel for families easier by staking out a trail across the country of Brethren households available for bed and breakfast. Many of the host homes were those of older adults with rooms to spare and time to be hospitable.

In another community a program for out-of-town family members visiting hospitalized relatives was started by the hospital's Pink Ladies team (mostly older women) who knew peers nearby with houses now shorn of family of their own. Owners who were willing to become hosts and hostesses were given guidance for opening their homes to paying guests. They also received training in responding to persons in bereavement.

The need for voluntary service in our society is as wide as the imagination can conceive. The Shepherd's Center in Kansas City, Missouri, is a Methodist program that matches the skills of senior volunteers with needs in the community. In England, where cash flow is generally much less than in the United States, the parishes have instituted Barter Societies. An older man will dig the garden in exchange for some of the landlady's canned produce after the crop is harvested. A crippled woman will care for two small children in exchange for their mother's doing her shopping and laundry. Once a month everyone involved in the Barter Society goes to church and stays for a small meal with the rest of the folks.

In the United States our approximation of the Barter Society is the self-help group movement. About 3,000 self-help groups now exist, with members helping one another by providing friendly support, understanding, skills, practical information, and the kind of consolation and encouragement that can be given by someone who "has been there." These groups recognize that everyone needs support systems and that systems we had long counted on are now eroding because of changes in society, new family patterns, legislation, and various factors beyond our control. These "talk-it-over" and "lend-a-hand" groups are voluntary. They meet in churches, community centers, and homes, sometimes with a professional person invited to provide special training. But for the most part, members help one another, as friends do, by drawing on their own accumulated resourcefulness.[9]

The role of teacher's helper in some public schools attracts older volunteers. Their stories are sometimes poignant. A lonely, widowed retiree responded to a local school's SOS for helpers. He was assigned to a class whose teacher suggested, "Come and just be around, take it as it happens." One day a withdrawn 8-year-old girl attached herself to him, saying nothing but staying close. Eventually, in bits and pieces, she told her story of sexual abuse, physical neglect, and isolation in her own home. Thanks to this quietly listening grandfather, the child was rescued. Another child, a hyperactive boy who when left alone could not concentrate enough to learn, found a friend in an older volunteer who sat with him and calmly, patiently talked with him. In this aura of quiet, loving, daily attention the boy could do his work and learn.

Older volunteers have the gifts of time and love to share. From them the emotionally disturbed, affection-starved, acting-out children who can turn a classroom into turmoil may receive the attentive care they need—care that cannot be bought.

Concern for the quality of education is prominent in the conversation of a church retirement community on the West Coast. An 84-year-old said, "Let's not just talk about it, let's do something about it!" There now exists a "writing alliance" between a group of retirees interested in writing and an equal number of young people from a nearby school. They meet regularly to share their work and critique it. Comradery, mutual respect, and self-esteem are nurtured in this intergenerational venture. In addition, the art of writing, grossly neglected today, gets good support. We underscore this experience as an excellent illustration of how a value recognized as important by the senior generation can be activated in the young when the two generations experience it together.

Many older adults find gratification and meaning in reaching out to others in a wide variety of services and supportive enterprises. Others, in numbers gradually increasing, are involving themselves in issues and situations where political, social, institutional, or legal change is necessary to assure justice and peace at home and abroad and to further the public good. Older people with discretionary time are sitting in on city council and school board meetings and in sessions of environmental protection agencies and public-health boards, to check chicanery or to further much needed two-way communication between such agencies and the general public. Still others organize for public attention and change, and an increasing number serve as community "watchdogs."

Two retired men, one concerned about what is happening to our trees and the other a skilled fisherman concerned about polluted water and streams, spoke of their interests with several Boy Scout troops. As a result some of the scouts became the nucleus of the organization Young Citizens Concerned. This is "generativity" at work in the best of ways, young and old together caring about God's world.

Many religious groups and individuals concerned about public affairs, ecology, health, and other issues find that the adult courses developed by the American Association of Retired Persons are excellent resources available at little or no cost, ready for leaders in churches, local libraries, and clubs to use. A retired high school principal responded to one of these, the 55-Alive driver training program designed to help senior citizens be safe drivers. He corralled 25 retired colleagues from church and school contacts to set up the course in four Illinois counties. Now it has spread throughout the state. Many state legislatures assure a 10% reduction in insurance premiums to those who pass the AARP driving course. The 55-Alive program was conceived by older people for older people, and it is taught by them. The initial Illinois law was passed as a result of lobbying by older citizens. Older adults in action to save lives! AARP driver training is now available in all states.

Most of our denominations maintain a Washington, D.C., office for government relations, with some of their work done by volunteers. Older adults apply for these positions, which provide excellent training in legislative and political processes, valuable preparation for leadership roles back home where voting counts. The elderly have a larger percentage of voters than any other age group. In addition to the voting box, there is always the mailbox, an implement increasingly used for today's participation in sociopolitical change. Human justice and world survival issues merit much more attention than they usually receive in the churches. Where are the elderly as active agents in creating a better future? Is this their role? We affirm it is uniquely their role. Their disestablishment is a gift, an opportunity to dream of a new order, to pursue visions of new structures and ways of functioning as well as new alliances to replace the tightening knots of injustice and self-concern, discrimination, and greed.

As they emerge from cocoons of dependency and self-doubt, the aging begin to become themselves—persons with strong instincts for the good of coming generations, with compassion for humanity deepened by their own losses and suffering through the years. They are clear about the futility of relying on material and physical realities for dependable security or salvation, and they are old enough to have experienced through repeated wars the madness of the military approach to world peace. We have among us many models of the integrity, the courage, and the faithful selflessness of Spirit-led older persons. They come from all cultures and every economic level. Let us form the most heterogeneous groupings we can, to learn to hear each other, to discover the contributions each can make to further the freedom and well-being of all people. Who and what can stop older adults? Nothing except their own lethargy. God has given to generous numbers the privilege of surviving—a gift to be used for the larger creation, not just in self-interest.

By the year 2020 there will be 40 million people over the age of 60 in the United States and nearly 600 million in the world. If we exist at all by then, mobilization for a new world order will be under way *by negotiation*. We believe "that the new world order can be promoted by older people, the group most free to do it."[10] If the ministry of older people can become prophetic as well as existential, older members then can serve the world as the Spirit's instruments of social transformation. We return to Nicodemus: Can an old person be reborn?

As God wrestled with Jacob and David, so the Spirit seeks to wrestle with us to the very end, winning us from ego-centeredness to Christ Jesus' way of life.

As surely as God gives gifts to the elderly, the elderly are intended to give gifts of themselves to the world.

It is the role of the churches to nurture the ministries of their members, whatever their age.

Notes

1.   Ernest G. Hall, "Spirituality During Aging" (Paper presented at the Thirty-sixth Annual Scientific Meeting of the Gerontological Society of America, San Francisco, 1983).

2.   "The Spectacular Sixties," *Modern Maturity,* (December 1983): 55-58.

3.   *Discover Your Gifts,* Workbook, Christian Reformed House Missions, Grand Rapids, MI 49560, 1983.

4.   John Koenig, "The Older Persons' Worth: A Theological Perspective," Symposium at Union Theological Seminary (New York: Presbyterian Senior Services, 1980).

5.   Ibid.

6.   William Barclay, *The Gospel of John,* Vol. 1, Philadelphia: Westminster Press, 1975, 125.

7.   C. W. Peckham and A. B. Peckham, *I Can Still Pray* (Lebanon, Ohio: Otterbein Home, 1979). (Out of print.)

8.   Write Family Friends, Project Director, 409 Third Avenue S.W., Second Floor, Washington, DC 20024.

9.   Write New Jersey Self-Help Clearinghouse Nationwide, Saint Clare's Hospital, 6 Hinchman Avenue, Denville, NJ 07834.

10.   Jim Baines, "Aging and World Order," *The Whole Earth Papers,* No. 13, Global Education Association.

Study Guide

Challenge to Ministry: Opportunities for Older Persons

Reflection Questions

• Benignus identifies several biblical elders who were "called to the fore" when God wanted to bring about significant change. Can you think of modern-day elders who played a role in significant change? Why do you think older people are well suited for this role? What inhibits them or encourages them to take on the role of bringing about change?

• Koenig says that "God chooses old people as bearers and proclaimers of the New Creation. They are visionaries, futurists, people charismatically gifted with a clearer picture of God's unfolding plan than their younger brothers and sisters." How might older people use this gift in today's world? What do older people need to perform this ministry and how might others encourage and support them in it? What can/will you do?

• What are some of the illusionary "saviors" you cling to or have clung to in the past? How does one "let go" of these illusions and "abandon one's self to faith?"

• What are some of the gifts of older people you have experienced? In what ways do older adults in your congregation minister to others in the congregation or community? In what ways are their gifts intentionally used and acknowledged? What could your congregation do to be more intentional about supporting the ministries of older adults? What can/will you do to make that happen?

• The PBS radio series entitled "Late Bloomers," with Connie Goldman, features older adults who have begun new ventures in late life. If you were to be a late bloomer, what new venture might you begin (perhaps a career aspiration disregarded in your younger years, or a skill you always wanted to develop)? How might you begin? Whom might you contact to provide consultation or other resources? Spend some time in prayer about this germ of a "call" from God, and follow as you are led.

Group Process

Purpose: To identify new opportunities for older adults and ways for congregations to develop and support the ministries of older adults.

Step 1:   Group members skim the chapter and choose one illustration that excites them or with which they can identify.

Step 2:   In small groups, invite each participant to tell his or her choice and say why it is a model. At what point does it speak to hopes and wishes for future development?

Step 3:   The author suggests that our older years are a new age with new spiritual potential for us as visionaries, prophets, change agents acting to bring about God's new order. Ask each small group to make two lists in response to these questions:

  •   Considering the stories you chose, what are some of the characteristics of the new age? What other characteristics would you add to the list?

  •   What are some of the stumbling blocks you can identify in society and in the church that would hinder the movement of older adults into the new age?

Step 4:   Ask each small group to bring its two lists to the larger group, post them, and read them aloud. Ask the entire group to make another list in response to this question:

  •   What transformations in your congregation's life and environment would make it more possible for older persons to manifest the wishes and visions of the new age?

Step 5:   Ask the group to identify one or two items on the list that they feel they can and want to implement. List the necessary action steps, including what needs to happen, who needs to be involved, what will it cost (time, supplies, and money), where resources can be found, when each step will be completed, how participants will communicate with one another during the process, and how they will celebrate.

Alternative

Step 5:   (For groups with members of more than one congregation.) Write, individually or as a group, a rite of passage for the movement from the time of employment to the years of "retirement," or from the "active household" to the "empty nest."

Meditation and Prayer

Nancy Roth

In Norwich, England, nestled beside the Church of St. Julian, there is a small chapel that has become a shrine for the many pilgrims who come to pay homage to one of Norwich's most noted citizens, Dame Julian, the fourteenth-century mystic and woman of prayer. The chapel is the site of the cell or "anchorhold" (the term for the dwelling of a religious recluse or "anchoress"), where Julian lived for almost 50 years. This small sanctuary provides a helpful symbol for prayer at any age, but particularly in our final years.

Two windows are cut into the whitewashed walls of Julian's cell. One window, looking into the church of St. Julian, gave the anchoress a clear view of the altar. On the wall opposite, a window looks out onto what was one of the busiest streets in the city. Through that window, men and women in need of Julian's prayers shared their concerns, joys, and tragedies with the wise anchoress. The rhythm of Julian's life danced between these windows. She gazed toward the infinite, eternal reality of God expressed in the worship inside the church, and also toward the holiness of God incarnate discovered in the daily life that bustled outside. Julian, although she did not move beyond a cell approximately 100 feet square, was not disconnected from life.

Each of us is a "Julian cell," with the need for a similar rhythm: to gaze toward God and toward our neighbors. It is easy to ignore this truth in the ebullient years of youth and the hectic years of middle age. But one of the gifts of moving on through life is an increasing recognition of our need to build our relationship to God through prayer, as well as maintaining our relationship to other people.

Long life itself can shrink our worlds; our energy may decline or we

41

may become subject to physical limitations that dictate our living space be no larger than Julian's small cell. But our circumstances need not limit either the richness of our inner lives nor our connections with the outside world.

As we gaze inward, at any age—"toward the altar"—we seek a framework for our particular time of life, and also for our final earthly passage, our dying. The first step in discovering this framework can be provided by asking the question, "Who am I?" A profoundly Christian answer to that question is found in a dramatic vignette contained in the second chapter of Genesis. There, God is pictured as a sculptor who scoops up a handful of earth (in the Hebrew, *adamah*), molds a human form (*adam*), and breathes life (*ruach*) into the creation. So we (*adam*) are *adamah* plus *ruach*: earth animated by God's life-giving breath. You have noticed, of course, the Hebrew pun!

Certainly, we have all experienced ourselves as *adamah*. Our bodies refuse to be ignored. Whether we have colic as newborns, chicken pox as 8-year-olds, acne as adolescents, hypertension as adults, or cataracts as elders, we are continuously reminded of our earthliness. Moreover, our physical well-being, or the lack of it, makes a profound impact upon our mental well-being. Religions that urge us to despise or ignore our bodies just do not work for us, either in a practical sense or in the theology that proclaims the Incarnation—God become flesh—as a central truth.

But we are more than our bodies. In Genesis, we are told that the "something more" is *ruach*, God's life-breath itself. An increased sense of God's *ruach* in us can help us cope with any decline we may encounter in the well-being of our physical selves, or *adamah*. (Research has proven this to be true even on a purely medical level.)

The increased leisure of our later years is likely to provide us with an opportunity to discover the "space" within us that longs for God. It may begin as a feeling of loneliness, emptiness, or uselessness; but, finally, this "space" can lead us to the desire that is like a "magnetic attraction" for our Creator. "You have made us for Yourself," said St. Augustine of Hippo, "and our hearts are restless until they rest in You." We may have tried to find other ways to satisfy our restlessness during our energetic middle years—money, fame, power, a sense of usefulness—but those cannot permanently satisfy us.

The story of Genesis 2 reminds us that our ultimate identity rests not in our function in the workplace or in society, but in who we are in relation to God. It is an identity that we discover ever more deeply in prayer, an identity that cannot ever be taken away from us, either in life or in death.

Who am I? I am *adamah*, animated by *ruach*. I share that identity with every other human being in the world. And yet how different we all are from one another! Our *adamah* can be pictured as not only our physicality but also the raw material of our personalities, our gifts and our shortcomings. It is *our adamah*, not anyone else's, that God wishes to animate with life-breath, whatever our circumstances, whatever our age.

Genesis 2:7 prefigures St. Paul's admonition, "Your body is a temple of the Holy Spirit" (1 Cor. 6:19). Today Paul would write to us, "You are the *church* (or chapel, or cathedral) of the Holy Spirit." I find that reminder very comforting as I grow older. For when I ask myself *why* the great churches of Europe, which I love to visit, are such holy places, I realize that *age* is what has made them so glorious. The beautiful architecture is only a kind of reliquary for the real treasure: the centuries of prayer and worship that have created an atmosphere of *ruach* one can enter as almost a physical reality, like plunging into the sea. We as individuals do not have centuries—only a lifetime—to discover the holiness that dwells within us as a gift from God. "I in them and you in me, that they may become completely one, so that the world may know that you have sent me and have loved them even as you have loved me" (John 17:23). *I in them.* We all know the beautiful elderly who reflect such love. Their lined faces, like the worn stone steps into a cathedral sanctuary, are living evidence of a life's pilgrimage with God.

Like the life within the walls of Julian's cell, the life of prayer is a rhythm—a pattern of giving and receiving, of going within ourselves and of reaching outside ourselves. Most of us have discovered the inevitability of this rhythm in our lives. Perhaps we have reached a point of fatigue that made us fight for some time alone. Or we have let ourselves become so isolated that we are ravenously hungry for human contact.

Times of prayer and meditation are a deliberate return to the space at the center of our beings where we are in touch with our deepest selves, in relationship with God and with the world. Like Julian, we attempt to dwell at the center, poised between two "windows" and trying to move between them without stumbling. We try to let the light from each window lead us toward the vista the other provides for us: praying at the church window does not isolate us from others any more than leaning on the windowsill into the street makes us forget God. The ways we honor these two relationships will change as we age. We can pray for the wisdom to make these changes with imagination and grace, knowing that God understands our limitations and circumstances better than we ourselves.

There are as many ways to pray, or to grow in relationship with God, as there are ways to grow in friendship with other human beings. We can use words (verbal), thought (reflective prayer), silence (contemplative prayer), or action. Most people feel an affinity for one or another of these kinds of prayer, but it is helpful to know them all, for then eventually prayer can become a way of living rather than a specific activity—an underlying consciousness of God's presence within us and with us in every moment of our lives.

Preparation for Prayer

In order for you to pray, especially if you are beginning to incorporate specific prayer times into your daily schedule, you need to make sure that your life has some breathing space. You will need *privacy*: a space where you will not be interrupted. You will need to set aside *time*: a space, anywhere from 15 minutes to an hour, when you will not think of other duties. Equally important, especially in this fast-paced culture, is a state of inner relaxation, or psychological space.

It is helpful to begin your prayer time with focusing on the body, for physical tension often gets in the way of our attentiveness to God. The following exercises may be helpful. Use those that suit you, bearing in mind that these are not calisthenics; the goal is to focus the mind and heart. If you have any physical problems, modify these exercises according to your doctor's advice. You may repeat each exercise as often as you wish.

Either standing or sitting in a straight chair, stretch toward the ceiling with both arms as you inhale, then exhale and let the arms drop.

Let the head drop forward. Relax the neck, and roll the head gently toward the right shoulder; then roll the head forward again, and toward the left shoulder. Roll the head forward again, and then raise it as if someone were pulling an imaginary string attached to the top of the skull.

Raise the shoulders up toward the ears, bring them back, down, and forward, making a circle. Reverse the circle.

There are many other exercises that will help you feel quiet. Some people discharge the physiological "static" of life through activities such as walking or swimming before they settle down to pray.

Now choose a comfortable position for prayer, in which you will feel relaxed yet alert. Some people like to sit on a chair, feet flat on the floor or crossed at the ankles, with their hands palms up on the lap.

Be aware of the weight of your body and of your breathing. Breathe through your nostrils, trying to breathe as naturally as an infant breathes, expanding the abdomen and whole rib cage area as you inhale, and letting it fall as you exhale.

Picture the tension draining from each part of the body in turn, beginning with your feet, right up to the face and skull (the right foot, the right calf, the right thigh, the left foot, etc.).

Verbal Prayer

Verbal prayer is prayer with words—your own or the words of others. The English teacher of prayer Evelyn Underhill kept a notebook of prayers she especially loved. You may wish to create such a notebook or to use prayers found in a book of worship. Such use of the words of others helps us remember that our prayers, even when said in private, are part of a great community stretching across the world and across the centuries.

Honest conversation with God covers the whole spectrum of our life. There is nothing we need hold back: God understands our anger, our depression, our desires, and our sorrows, as well as our joys and thanksgivings. This conversation need not be confined to specific prayer-time, but can be interwoven throughout your day's activities; as one of my friends calls it, "an ongoing chat."

- ## An exercise in verbal prayer

Adoration: Begin your prayer time with adoration: acknowledging the holiness of God with awe, wonder, and love. Acknowledge God's nearness to you, the God who is beyond anything you can imagine.

Praise: Remember times in your life when you have had a sense of God's presence and care. How did you feel then? Like singing or dancing?

Thanksgiving: For what specific things do you give thanks to God? Your family, your friends, or the memories associated with them? The earth's beauty and complexity? A measure of good health? The loving care of other people? The knowledge of God's love for you as revealed in the gift of Jesus Christ?

Oblation (self-giving): Offer yourself for the working out of God's purposes. Reflect on whether you accept yourself. God wants you as you are, as well as the person you can become with God's help.

Intercession (prayer for others): There are so many needs in the world that you may feel overwhelmed. Try to discover what needs particularly move you. They may be international in scope (some people pray with the front page of the newspaper before them), or those of a personal list of people you feel called to hold before God. As you become increasingly sensitive to the life of the Spirit working within you, you will find this kind of prayer becoming more and more spontaneous: a quiet prayer for the homeless woman you pass on the city street, for the victims of the disaster you see on the evening television news, or for the grandson you are worried about.

Intercession helps us understand the *communion of saints;* it is a way of talking about our unity with other people, both in life and in death. Some people have had the experience of becoming quiet in preparation for prayer and finding the thought of another person coming into their minds, along with a desire to pray for that person. Such an occurrence gives us a hint about what we mean when we say that God prays in us. We begin to realize that somehow, in a way beyond human understanding, intercession—indeed, all prayer—is our cooperation with God, that it is our way of helping "God's will be done" in the world.

In your later years, you may find time for intercessory prayer with other people. Intercessory prayer groups, in parishes or in retirement communities, meet regularly to pray for the needs of the world. You do not even need to meet in person. You can form a prayer chain with others, in which you distribute by mail or communicate on the telephone the concerns you will pray for. In my own parish, there is a small but devoted group, which includes both an octogenarian and a nonagenarian, who meet for morning prayer and intercessions every weekday at 8:00 A.M. Other parishioners use the parish bulletin's intercession list for daily prayers in their homes. You may not have a window looking out onto the busiest street in your town as Julian did, but you can contribute to the well-being of the world in this simple and meaningful way nevertheless.

Petition (prayer for your own needs): What do you *really* need? Place your life, your needs, your fears, and your complaints before God. You need hold nothing back, for God knows all these things anyway.

Penitence: This is a prayer asking for healing as well as forgiveness. One way to approach this prayer is to think about what impedes God's life-breath moving through you. Lack of self-worth? Wrong priorities? Deliberate sin? Thoughtlessness? Past resentments that need to be healed? Accept God's healing forgiveness, which is waiting for you. Also ask God to help you forgive others.

Trust: End your prayer by quietly placing before God all your thoughts, feelings, anxieties, and hopes. You might think of this prayer of trustfulness as a deep, relaxed breath or sigh of relief.

Reflective Prayer

Reflective prayer is the prayer that moves beyond words, usually through *thinking* about the meaning of a passage of Scripture. One traditional method of doing this is called *lectio divina.*

• **Prayer Exercise:** *Lectio Divina*

Choose a passage from the Bible and set aside at least 20 minutes. Read the passage slowly. If a phrase or word commands your attention, stop reading. Dwell on the word or phrase. Let it become a "window" through which the life-breath of God can enter your life. Spend as long as you wish; when you feel ready, read on, pausing again when you are drawn to do so.

During the sixteenth century, a more complex process of reflection on scripture was developed. The best-known form of this type of reflective prayer, developed by St. Ignatius Loyola, is called Ignatian meditation. A simple way to move through Ignatius' basic structure is to remember four words: *prepare, picture, ponder,* and *permit.*

• **Prayer Exercise: Modified Ignatian Meditation**

Prepare. The night before you plan to do this meditation, choose a passage of Scripture on which to reflect—preferably a story from the Old or New Testament that contains a scene you can picture. Read it over slowly before you go to bed.

The next day, at the time you have set aside for prayer (I would suggest at least 20 minutes), relax physically by using some of the suggested exercises if they are helpful. Silently offer this time to God and read the selected passage over again slowly.

Picture. Try to experience the story as if you were present. In preparation for this part of the prayer, some people find it helpful to consult a biblical commentary or other study resource. The more you know about the social and literary background of the story, the better. Above all, use your imagination, including the senses of sight, hearing, smell, taste, and touch.

Ponder. Does the passage give you some kind of message about your own life? Is there a phrase that strikes you? Do you identify with a particular person or emotion in the story?

Permit. This is when you ask yourself the question, "How can I respond in some way to what I have understood about this passage?" The response could be an action as simple as writing a letter, making a phone call, or finishing a long-neglected task. It may be a change of heart about someone who has been irritating you. It may be a prayer for forgiveness or of thanksgiving. It may a decision to keep a particular phrase in your mind throughout the day.

Conclude this Ignatian meditation exercise with a quiet time during which you give thanks for God's presence with you.

The Ignatian method of reflection may be based on content other than scripture. For example, you may reflect on a natural object. Especially if you are housebound, this is a wonderful way to connect with God's creation.

Prepare: Find a shell, stone, pine cone, leaf, or other natural object that captures your fancy. *Picture:* Hold the object and use all your senses to explore it, imagining that you are a child discovering it for the first time. *Ponder:* What specifically strikes you? What memories does the object evoke? Does it suggest some message about your life? *Permit:* How might this meditation be expressed through an action or change of attitude?

Some people reflect on their dreams in this way. Other subject matter for reflection might be works of art, poetry, music, devotional writings, and incidents in your life. In fact, this would be a good format to use in writing a journal. Many people have found that habitually recording their thoughts, feelings, and memories in writing is a helpful way to pray. It also provides some time to savor the memories of the past and the events of each day, as well as a means of reflecting on them. With pencil or pen in hand, or with typewriter or computer under the fingers, you can record your own responses to the questions, "What do I feel? What do I think? What do I remember? What is God saying to me in my life?"

Contemplative Prayer

During some of your prayer times, you may have experienced a moment of just resting in God's presence, without any "thinking" going on. This is the mode of prayer the Christian tradition calls contemplative prayer, although sometimes today it is called meditation. My favorite description of this prayer occurs in a story about a French

priest, who, curious about a peasant whom he has seen kneeling in his
little parish church for hours at a time, finally asks him what he does
while he is praying. "Why, it's very simple," the peasant replies. "I just
look at God, and God looks at me."

In spite of the apparent simplicity of contemplation as I have just
described it, past Christian tradition has tended to consider it a form
most suitable for those who are very "advanced" in prayer. But *everyone* is potentially a contemplative, for becoming attentive and responsive to the presence of God is what we were created for—why we are
"restless" for God, in St. Augustine's words. Our yearning for the experience of contemplation may be what accounts for the present popular-
ity of Eastern spiritualities and their secular offshoots. These
spiritualities usually teach useful techniques of meditation or contemplative prayer, and the Christian church has been enriched by exposure
to them.

Contemplation requires a measure of interior silence we may not
previously have associated with prayer. However, most of us can probably remember "contemplative moments" in our lives, when our minds,
however briefly, became peaceful and we were able to just "rest" in the
present moment. In contemplative prayer, the moments of such quiet-
ness often come and go. Thoughts will inevitably flit across our minds,
like birds on the horizon, and our attention must be gently brought
back.

It is important to realize that you are not likely to have the sense of
accomplishment in this type of prayer that you may have felt in verbal
prayer or reflective prayer. It is rather like the desert, in contrast to the
bustling city. You may at times have a powerful sense of the presence
of God; at other times, you may experience emptiness, or simply faithful waiting. Contemplation demands trust in the goodness of the One
whom we are seeking, and the courage and willingness to open ourselves to God's love and acceptance. This is, therefore, not only the
simplest but also the most difficult of the ways to pray—because it
means giving up our own control. It is also potentially the most transforming of prayers. We might call contemplative prayer a "school of
love," for as we rest in the presence of a loving God, we ourselves grow
in the ability to love not only God, but also ourselves and other people.

• **Prayer Exercise: Contemplation**

In exploring this way of praying, I suggest that you spend 5 to 10 minutes quieting the body and the mind, then another 20 minutes in silence, focusing on whatever you have chosen, using some of the ideas that follow and knowing that the true focus is on the presence of God. The mind should not feel tense but relaxed; thoughts may come and go, but don't feel anxious about them. Simply offer this space in your life to "just look at God" as "God looks at you." You may wish to explore this way of prayer in the company of others, as well as alone. People who gather in a group for contemplative prayer attest to the tremendous power of the communal silence.

A simple format for contemplative prayer includes *preparation, finding a focus*, and *passing beyond the focus*.

Preparation: Stretch, relax, and find a position in which your body is comfortable—but not so comfortable that you will go to sleep! Begin always with awareness of your body and awareness of your breath, keeping in mind the image of God's life-breath breathing through you. Let your mind relax, and quietly offer this time to God.

Focus: You may wish to experiment over the course of some weeks with various ways of focusing the mind. Some people are oriented toward movement, some toward words, some toward images, others toward what they touch or hear or smell. In reading my suggestions, bear in mind that learning about prayer reveals the incredible variety of human psychological makeup. Choose what is helpful and seems to lead you to God; gently leave behind what does not feel appropriate for you.

Focus on the breath: This will appeal to the kinetically oriented, those who naturally experience life through movement. Center your attention on your breathing; think of God's breath as moving through you, and think of yourself as breathing in God's life and love and giving it back to God.

Focus on a mantra: A mantra is a word or phrase used as a focus in contemplative prayer. In using a mantra, you may coordinate the word or phrase with your breath. Your mantra may express something about your relationship to God. It may be simply the word

"God." It may be "Come Holy Spirit" on the inhalation and "I give myself to you" on the exhalation. A classic mantra is the "Jesus Prayer" of the Eastern Orthodox tradition: "Lord Jesus Christ, have mercy on me." Scripture, particularly the Psalms, contains many potential mantras; choose a phrase that combines meaning with rhythm, such as "Be still and know that I am God."

Focus on an image: Some people find it easiest to focus on an image. Picture in your imagination a scene, indoors or outdoors, where you have been aware of God's presence. Or picture our Lord, a symbolic shape, or a light. You may also actually *look* at a religious painting, a crucifix, a candle, or something that draws your attention and takes it God-ward. The tradition of icons in the Eastern church grew out of the practice of using such paintings as windows through which one gazed at the divine. A natural object, such as a stone or sea shell, may become a focus for attention as you rest in the presence of the Creator.

Other points of focus: *Touch*—Exploring with your fingers the texture, weight, and shape of a natural object or a religious symbol such as a rosary or crucifix. *Listening*—Chanting, or listening to music or to the sounds around you as if *they* were music. *Smell*—Incense, flowers, or a pine grove, for example. *Taste*—Fresh-baked bread or a single raisin, eaten slowly. All these methods demonstrate the reality of our *adamah*: that our senses can help us to grow in our relationship to God.

Passing beyond the focus: There may come a time when you will want to move beyond the focus you have chosen and just become silent in God's presence. At those moments, permit yourself to just *be* in the present, without analyzing the experience. When your mind begins to wander again, as it inevitably will, return gently to the focus you have chosen.

Some Miscellaneous Thoughts

The life of prayer includes both deliberate times of prayer and times when your life's activities themselves become prayerful. Like the five-finger exercises that prepare for the piano sonata, or the barre exercises that warm up the dancer's muscles for ballet, intentional prayer time deepens the relationship with God that frees us to be our truest selves in our daily lives. Prayer can be seen as the *center* of each day, as it is a return to our "center"—our true identity as creatures of God. Our ongoing consciousness of this truth has been called "habitual recollection"—literally, a *re*-collection of ourselves. It is the opposite of being scattered.

The following are some suggestions that might help us on our way, especially as we explore what prayer means to us in the "third age" of life.

Spiritual friendship: If you are part of a worshiping community (a church or a prayer group), you may already know the support that mutual prayer can give. Another way of connecting with others is to have a "spiritual friend" with whom you can compare notes, perhaps sharing reflections or journal entries and scheduling a time of silent prayer together. You may even wish to seek an experienced spiritual director for guidance. The tradition of spiritual direction is an ancient one in which interest has recently revived. A skilled spiritual director combines knowledge of the Christian tradition of prayer with openness to the Spirit. Especially in a culture that tends to devalue the gifts of the elderly, we need to walk together as we seek our true identities as the men and women we are in relation to God.

Spiritual books and tapes: These can connect us with kindred spirits and add a rich dimension to prayer. Many of us have had the experience of feeling that a favorite author is a special friend, although we may never have communicated in person. Many current religious books are also available on tape. Music on tape is also a wonderful prayer resource. In this area, the choice is a very individual matter, but I cannot help but mention the wonderful chants from the Taizé Community. The local parish church may have a library from which you can borrow, or you may wish to put yourself on the catalog list of a religious publishing house or bookstore.

Journals and autobiographies: We spoke earlier about recording events, thoughts, and prayers in a journal. The writing of an autobiography is another form of journaling, dealing with the past rather than the present. It is a marvelous way to delve into our memories; I have found that beginning to write about a past era of my life evokes, slowly but surely, many of the rich details I had thought forgotten. Looking back over our lives can help us to see God's healing, comforting, supporting presence throughout our years. It opens our eyes to the value of our lives, as we see how our lives have touched others, and others' lives have touched ours. Our lives, indeed, are a "work of art."

It is important to add that we need not *write* a journal or autobiography; in these days of wondrous technology, we need only press the "record" button on a tape recorder and speak aloud our thoughts and memories. Indeed, our voice will add a personal dimension to our living history not possible with the written word alone.

Reaching out to others: Many of us have talents we can use to reach out to others: knitting, drawing, or other skills. But we have special opportunities in our older years to use an intangible skill: the gift of friendship, especially with those younger than we are. I have always noticed the special affinity between my mother and my children: no "generation gap" there; rather, a "generation bond." We may not feel "useful" when we are merely listening to the concerns of a younger person, but we are. Listening ears are hard to find in this day and age. Whether we are supportive companions to friends of our own generation, by letter, by phone, or in person, or occasional baby-sitters for people many years younger, we have a gift to give: ourselves. Mary, a friend in her 80s who was once an invalid herself, has for years written letters to children who are hospitalized or housebound. She calls her effort "The Chuckle Club," and she has friends and fans all over the map, many of them now grown to adulthood. Even if we are shut-ins, we can minister through "Julian's window on the world."

Kindness: Another way of connecting through that "window" is to take the opportunities we already *have* for human interchange and to see them as sacred. My friend Katherine, in declining health, moved to a nursing home. Instead of railing against the fate that removed her from her sphere of usefulness and community, she became the "talking books" coordinator for the home's sight-impaired residents. Later, when she could no longer do that, her kindness was expressed through her attitude toward those who cared for her. This is no mean feat when one is in declining health, for unlike the picture painted in romantic novels, illness and extreme old age do *not* automatically bring along with them sweetness of temperament. Most of us will probably reach the point when the only way we can pray "through action" is through a smile or kind word to overworked and fatigued care-givers or family.

Preparation for dying: You have probably seen paintings of medieval saints seated at their desks, pondering a skull. This practice was intended to remind the saint that eternal life lay beyond the *adamah*, which was earthly and temporary. Although it is not a popular activity in our society to contemplate death in this way, recognizing that our *adamah* is a temporary part of us and that fullness of life lies beyond it can be a profound spiritual practice. We need not contemplate bones to do that, for many other, more practical opportunities are open to us. My parish offers its people a useful booklet called *Planning for Burial from a Christian Point of View*, in which there are sections for autobiographical information (for the obituary, one assumes), estate information, instructions for the funeral and for burial, and procedural instructions for the survivors. Facing one's own death through looking at these questions can be a liberating activity. Such simple actions as choosing the hymns for one's funeral, making a list of possessions for our family, or signing a Living Will, can help us move on in life without illusion, recognizing each day as a gift from God.

Theophane, a Russian bishop of the nineteenth century, describes prayer as "standing before God with the mind in the heart." We have seen prayer as a process of moving from words to reflection to loving: from the mind to the heart. The last part of the process is surely our *living out* of our love, moving through all the phases of life, and beyond the gateway of death. Whatever we pray and however we pray, our prayer is an encounter with the Reality that is God. As we consciously return to our Center, again and again, we encounter the One who breathes life into us and gives us our deepest identities, which can never, by the events of life or by death, be taken from us. As we grow in relationship with that One in all the ways we pray, we become more and more certain that our adventure will be a never-ending one, in which we explore the joyous landscape that is the eternal life of God within our souls.

Study Guide

Meditation and Prayer

Reflection Questions

- When am I most aware of *adamah*? How does my body feel when I am anxious and afraid? Calm? Fatigued? Rested? Angry? Happy?

- When have I been aware of *ruach*?

  Has crisis, loss, or anxiety ever brought me face to face with an inner emptiness or yearning? Has that emptiness ever led me toward God?

  Do I remember times when I have been profoundly aware of God's life-breath within me, in response to an event, a person, or an experience of beauty?

- How would I describe my temperament (my personal characteristics, my gifts and shortcomings), my physical condition, and my life situation? Do I accept this raw material or *adamah,* or try to ignore or reject it? Can I think of ways in which God's *ruach* can give this *adamah* "new life"?

Group Process

Purpose: To identify difficulties in past prayer disciplines and to experience one or more prayer models. (Can be done in two to four-plus sessions using groups of five to eight persons.)

Step 1:   Ask each person to identify two or three difficulties experienced in private prayer life. Invite each person in turn to add one item to a group list until all difficulties have been identified. (Members can "pass" if their items are already listed or they don't want to participate.)

Step 2:   Give each small group the following questions and invite them to discuss them for 10 minutes.

Which ideas excited you? Seemed appropriate? Were new? Made you uncomfortable? Were there any models you have tried and rejected? Tried and found useful? Does any model seem to offer a way out of previous difficulties?

Step 3: Prepare two or three people to help you with this step—each will lead a group through one of the models. Invite participants to select a model to experience. Each leader should take his or her group to a room (or area) apart from the other groups. Each group should take 30 to 40 minutes to experience the prayer method. Ask the small groups to close their session without returning to the larger group. Encourage participants to continue using the chosen model in the coming week, and invite them to return and share reactions.

Step 4: When the group reconvenes, invite each small group to report back to the larger group. Discuss the following questions:

Was the experience what you hoped for? What changes would you make? Additions? What next steps would you take? What further helps would be useful?

If desired, return to small groups and repeat the process one or two more times so participants can experience the other methods.

**Alternate
Step 4:** Instead of or in addition to repeating the process, invite the group to discuss and/or try each of the suggestions at the end of the chapter. You might invite them to divide into groups according to interest or, if the groups are small enough, invite them to share stories of experiences they have had in each area (journals, spiritual friendship, etc.). See also the chapter by Eugene Bianchi later in this book.

The Gift of Wisdom

Robert W. Carlson

Aging and Wisdom

In the third act of Verdi's opera *Ernani*, the Spanish king Don Carlos is hiding in the tomb of his ancestor Charlemagne. His life is being threatened by his enemies, but, unknown to him, he is about to hear the signal that reveals that he has been chosen Holy Roman Emperor. In overwhelming sadness at the direction his life has taken, he sings:

> *Scepters! Riches! Honors! Beauties!*
> *Youth! What are you?*
> *Barks floating upon the sea of the years,*
> *which waves strike with constant troubles,*
> *until reaching the tomb's reef, your name*
> *plunges with you to nothingness!*
> *Oh, dreams and lying forms*
> *of my youthful years,*
> *if I believed in you too much,*
> *the spell now has vanished.*[1]

In his youth Don Carlos had harbored false dreams and illusions, illusions that life could bring unending happiness and fulfillment, dreams that relationships would last forever. Now, about to receive glory rather than death, he finds wisdom, wisdom that brings with it compassion for his adversaries and strength to rule his people.

While cleverness and intelligence may accompany youth, wisdom is usually associated with those of mature years. This is, of course, not universally true. The Bible, which often makes the association of wisdom and age, recognizes the tragedy of age without wisdom and the possibil-

58

ity of wisdom in one who is young. "Better," declares the author of Ecclesiastes, "is a poor but wise youth than an old but foolish king" (Eccles. 4:13). This truth is well illustrated in the apocryphal book of Susanna and the Elders, in which the two lecherous elders are exposed by the wise intervention of the young Daniel. Shakespeare, in *King Lear*, as if taking his text from the passage in Ecclesiastes cited earlier, exposes the tragedy of one who has become foolish in his old age. The aging monarch accepts the flattering but false words of his two daughters Goneril and Regan while rejecting the honest confession of the youngest, Cordelia. By so doing, he brings tragedy on himself and his entire household. The wisdom of age should have made Lear skeptical of flattery and aware that past actions are far more reliable guides to future behavior than easy assurances of undying love. Foolishness, however, prevails over wisdom, and death and sorrow ensue.

While wisdom does not come automatically with old age, wisdom seldom comes without the honing of life that long experience brings. Don Carlos's youthful illusions are like the illusions most of us held in our early years when life seemed simple, judgments black and white, goals obtainable by sincerity and hard work, relationships good or bad and relatively permanent. At some point, however, we discovered that some things are forever unobtainable, that despite the best intentions and heroic efforts, love and friendship do not always last, that good intentions are not always rewarded, that even good and religious people can disappoint and betray us. Wisdom is not just disillusionment with youthful values and aspirations; wisdom requires that we move beyond the limited perspectives of our youthful experience in order to see life in its larger perspective and wholeness. Wisdom and age do not increase in direct proportion to each other, but wisdom usually requires a good measure of life experience for its growth.

Wisdom also cannot be equated with accumulated information, or with the ability to produce beautiful works in music, sewing, carpentry, painting, or other creative fields, or even with the ability to do research and come up with new insights or new theoretical constructs. Wisdom is not something we attain by our strenuous efforts or our high intelligence. Wisdom may have been transmitted to us in a variety of ways, but it is fundamentally a gift of God. This does not mean that wisdom is exclusively manifest in religious people. Elements of wisdom and foolishness appear in both religious and nonreligious people, and the Bible is quite open about this fact. But in both the synagogue and the early church, wisdom is associated with age. The term of honor given to leaders is that of "elder." It is from the Greek word for elder that we derive our words presbyter and priest.

But what is wisdom? What does it mean to be wise? I asked this question in a class entitled "Ministry with and to Older People," a class of 14 seminary students and 12 people in their 60s and 70s.

I asked them to picture someone they know who is both old and wise, to talk with another person about the qualities they see in that wise man or woman, and then to share their observations. After that sharing and some discussion, we agreed upon the following list of qualities of our wise acquaintances:

1. They are still learning, open to change and new ideas.

2. They have had a great variety of experiences and are able to put them together.

3. They are secure enough in themselves to accept others despite differences of opinion or behavior.

4. They recognize their limitations and are comfortable in letting others know about them.

5. They are able to look forward to tomorrow rather than fear it.

6. They are able to see the positive side of things.

7. They know themselves and can communicate who they are to others.

8. They have the capacity to give to others.

9. They have an indefinable "something" that lets you go in to see them feeling "down" and to come out feeling "up."

10. They have the ability to be "with" other people, to have empathy.

11. They take care of themselves.

12. They have a wholistic approach to life.

13. They have a sense of humor, "a twinkle in their eyes."

This is only the product of 26 people engaging in a 50-minute exercise, but it helps focus on three important qualities of wisdom. The first is that wisdom involves one's total orientation to life, rather than the accumulation of specific knowledge or skills. Those of us who have spent years acquiring graduate degrees are not excluded from being counted among the wise, but we do not necessarily have an advantage over our less-learned peers. One of the people cited by the class members dropped out of school after the eighth grade but is still learning at 84. Wise people, it appears, have an openness to life that permits continued growth and continued appreciation of the new and the old, the familiar and the unfamiliar.

The second quality of wisdom my class members recognized is evidenced in the way we relate to others. Our wise elders had the ability "to give to others," "to have empathy," and "to accept others despite differences of opinion or behavior." This quality of wisdom was seen by both older and younger students as stemming from self-acceptance. As we accept ourselves, we are enabled to accept others. As we learn to love ourselves, we are freed to love others. One man in my class described his wife as a person who had grown wise with age. After joking about her ability to accept him and his "bad habits" through their 52 years of marriage, he became serious as he attributed her wisdom to her life in the church and years of volunteer work in her denominational home for the aged. She had grown wise through giving of herself to others. It would appear not only that wisdom enables us to relate well to others, but also that such relating and giving can in turn contribute to our growth in wisdom.

The third quality of wisdom identified by my class members is the ability to deal with the limits of life, either through faith acceptance or through humor. People who are wise know that their lives, their understanding, their years are limited. At times, the awareness of these limits may bring discouragement and despair, but, on the whole, wise people have learned to accept and even laugh at their limits. One octogenarian I met through a class member was a white water canoeist when he was in his 20s. As he became older, he told me, he switched to sailing on Lake Michigan. As he moved past middle age, he traded his sailboat for a power boat. "And now?" I asked. "Now," he responded with a smile, "I enjoy walking on the beach!"

Ego Integrity Versus Despair

One approach to our understanding of the nature of wisdom comes to us through the work of Erik Erikson. Erikson affirmed an important spiritual as well as psychological truth when he identified the task of the final stage of life as striking a balance between "ego integrity and despair."[2] He described this task as that of coming to terms with "one's one and only life cycle." In this stage we develop wisdom—the wisdom of perceiving our lives as whole and with wholeness, despite the brokenness we share with all other persons. The tension between ego integrity and despair is never fully resolved in this life, but the balance for the person of wisdom is on the side of integrity, wholeness.

Ego integrity versus despair, however, is a complex state that incorporates other life tensions, especially—but not uniquely—for the religious individual. Among the tensions are these: (1) between owning one's life and the recognition that we own nothing; (2) between seeing one's life as continuously interdependent upon the lives of others and as isolated, alone; (3) between grieving the increasing losses that accompany aging and trusting that these losses are redeemed and restored in the God who is the source and ground of all being.

Owning Our Lives and Recognizing That We Own Nothing

No matter what our views may be of life after death (unless we are convinced by claims of reincarnation), wisdom invites us to accept the life we are now leading, the life that began with our birth and will end with our death, as the one earthly life we have to live. We need to accept the burden and responsibility of our individual selves. Despite the exigencies of fate, the fortunes of my unique hereditary and environmental influences, my life is *my* responsibility and no one else's. One of the more difficult persons for pastors or counselors to help is the one who claims to be an innocent victim of others or of the fates. During the months in which this chapter was taking form, I was in the process of recovering from a broken ankle and other injuries received in an automobile accident. One of the things that disturbed me about my temporarily disabled state was the effect of my dependency on my approach to life. I became dependent on doctors, nurses, physical therapists, porters with wheelchairs in airports. It was a life stance that was both depressing and seductive to me: depressing because of the loss of power over my own life and activities and seductive because I found that I could fall into a pattern of relinquishing my personal responsibilities to others. After all, "What do you expect of a man with a broken ankle?" If I had not, somehow, been given the wisdom to meet as many of my commitments as I could manage, the time might have been even more difficult than it was, and I might have been an even more difficult patient! We need to own our own lives and relationships and the consequences of our choices and actions.

In tension with the necessary ownership of our own lives, however, is our recognition that we own nothing, and that we are simply stewards of our lives, our goods, and our relationships. One of the most beautiful chapels in the cathedral of Roskilde, the burial place of Danish monarchs, is the fifteenth-century chapel of Christian I. He and his Queen Dorothea are buried beneath simple slabs bearing their names. King Christian assumed that the chapel itself, a place for visitors to pray for, among other things, the repose of the monarchs' souls, was a sufficient memorial. The slabs, however, are now all but obscured by two immense alabaster and marble monuments bearing the carved images of two of Christian's descendants. In visiting this chapel I felt appreciation for the wisdom of a king who knew his limits, who knew that he, like all other people, was "from dust" and to dust he would return. I also felt amusement at the successors who spoiled the effect of the chapel with their ostentatious attempts to memorialize themselves with costly and elaborate tombs. To be sure, who among us has not felt the temptation to leave behind a monument or two to remind others of how great or good or, at least, how well intentioned we were? Who among us has the wisdom to be content with the simple slab acknowledging that we are as nothing before the grandeur of the Creator?

It is not just the temptation to believe that our ownership lasts beyond death that blocks our acquisition of wisdom. It is also the belief that even in this life we actually possess anything. One of the failings of our Western materialistic culture is our emphasis on possessing things. The shopping center has become the center of American life, and we often acquire things in order to "kill time," not realizing that time cannot be stopped or set back or reversed by our "getting and spending." I was recently struck by sadness as I joined a crowd of people pawing through goods at a garage sale, worldly goods being disposed of by the children after the death of their mother. "Getting and spending we lay waste our powers. . . ."[3]

Our acquisition of possessions is not limited to objects. It also includes people. Let me first say that I believe that human relationships, our close and intimate ties with friends and loved ones, are of the very essence of life. It is no accident that Jesus virtually equated neighbor love and love of God. To act, however, as if we possessed other persons—whether they be our friends, our children, our parents, or our spouses—is very different from love. A basic understanding of Christian stewardship is that we are set in this world as caretakers, as stewards, not as possessors. When we fall into the error of believing that we possess another person, our relationship becomes poisoned by a kind of idolatry in which we substitute ourselves for the One who alone possesses anything or anyone.

Wisdom, then, is putting aside the foolishness of believing that we possess anything, especially other persons. In a positive vein, it is coming to accept mortality in ourselves and others. It is coming to accept, at least in part or in some small beginning way, that for all the loving communion that may happen between myself and another, we are separate beings. What happens to that person may cause me pain and grief and shake the equilibrium of my life, but we ultimately belong not to each other but to the One in whom we "live and move and have our being."

To be wise, is, in one sense, to be a good steward. The Gospel story of the talents constitutes a plea for us to use what has been entrusted to us, but it is grounded in the truth that we own nothing, not even our lives.

Seeing One's Life as Interdependent on Others and as Isolated

Our lives are continuously interdependent on the lives of others and yet also isolated, alone. What we do affects others and what they do affects us. We, indeed, "do not live to ourselves" nor do we "die to ourselves" (Rom. 14:7). Both our living and dying are "to the Lord," as St. Paul observes. Our living and dying are also within a complex network of relationships and within a personal, family, and community history. The story of who I am includes the story of a host of other persons. It is a story I cannot tell without telling about them and about our interrelatedness, our shared joys and sorrows, our gains and losses, our hope and despair. To be wise is to know ourselves in our interdependence on others—others both living and dead. What I do or decide affects them, and in turn their actions affect my life, for good or ill.

Our dependence on others is illustrated by a story in the Talmud, a story about a traveler who saw a man planting a carob tree. The traveler asked the planter:

> How long does it take [for this tree] to bear fruit? The man replied: "Seventy years." He then further asked him: "Are you certain that you will live another seventy years?" The man replied: "I found [ready grown] carob trees in the world; as my forefathers planted them for me so I too plant these for my children."[4]

The storyteller then fell into a deep sleep for 70 years. When he awoke, he saw a man gathering the fruit of the carob tree, and he asked him, "Are you the man who planted the tree?" The man replied: "I am his grandson." We are debtors to our parents and grandparents for the trees from which we pick fruit, for the cities in which we live, for the art and literature and music we enjoy, for the discoveries that enrich our lives. In turn, we pass on to our heirs the fruit of our labor and imagination. Our lives are dependent on countless others, both those who have preceded us, and those among whom we live.

However, wisdom recognizes another truth, in tension with the truth about our interdependence: the truth that we are alone, separated from all others. No one can experience what we are experiencing in physical pain or pleasure, in emotional euphoria or agony. No one can live or die for us. In one sense, our life and death are solitary matters, and it is presumptuous for me or anyone else to say to you, "I know how you feel." It is wisdom to know that we are solitary, isolated individuals. It is a further step toward wisdom to be at some measure of peace with our aloneness, to know that not only can we live with that fearful truth, but that only in doing so can we discover at least one aspect of the truth of our unique being.

Grief and Redemption Accompanying Aging

Grieving is an essential part of life. The work of grief grows with age because of the increasing losses accompanying our aging. For many of us, this begins with the loss of the parents who bore and nurtured us and now leave us to be the older generation. Freud observed that the most important day in a man's life is the day his father dies. The same could be said of a woman in regard to her mother. This is not to minimize earlier childhood losses of friends and pets, familiar neighborhoods, and beloved teachers. We begin the grieving process early in life, perhaps as early as the day we give up our mother's breasts for other less personal sources of sustenance. The loss of parents, however, marks for most of us the beginning of a series of losses for which we must grieve and through grief learn to surrender what we once held close but now have lost.

In tension with grief is another stance toward life and its inevitable losses, the stance of trust or faith of believing that this loss is somehow redeemed in and by the God who is the source and ground of all people and things. We cannot, however, speak the word of faith lightly or glibly. Trusting and grieving are not alternative ways of reacting to loss, but are in tension, in coexistence with each other. To ask one in grief to exchange tears for faith is damaging and foolish advice. The men and women I know who have had the most difficulty in coming to terms with loss have usually been those who, because they mistakenly believed it to be right or virtuous, have denied their grief and put on a mantle of premature faith, saying such glib and pious words as, "It's no sense grieving. After all, we know that she is safe and with the Lord." At the right time, of course, these words are blessed words of faith, but at too early a time, as an escape from the necessary work of grief, they are harmful and diminish the wholeness that is wisdom.

The tension between grieving over our losses and accepting them in faith is illustrated in the novel *Flood*, by Robert Penn Warren. He develops his plot around a river town in Tennessee that is about to be inundated by the waters rising behind a newly constructed dam. The Baptist preacher, himself dying from cancer, plans a final service in his church that will both celebrate the death of their town and affirm that despite this death their individual and corporate lives have been blessed. The wisdom Brother Potts expresses is part of the wisdom of the aged, the wisdom to grieve our losses while trusting that they are in some strange way blessed, redeemed by God. The simple hymn Warren causes the preacher to compose affirms:

When I see the town I love
   Sinking down beneath the wave,
God, help me to remember then
   All the blessings that You gave.

When I see the life I led
   Whelmed and sunk beneath the flood,
Let the waters drown regret and envy—
   Make me see my life was good.[5]

The Gift to Be Shared

I began this chapter with a story about one king. I shall close with a story of another. Shortly after Solomon became king, we are told, God spoke to him in a dream and offered him a favor, saying, "Ask what I should give you" (1 Kings 3:5). Solomon, instead of asking for riches or power or honor, asked for wisdom. God, pleased at this choice, bestowed upon Solomon this gift and all the others as well. Solomon's choice pleased God because wisdom is a gift to be used for the well-being of others. Wisdom, while it is a precious gift to the individual, is always a gift to be shared, a light that cannot be "hidden under a bushel" but must be set forth for the good and enlightenment of others. It is conveyed, however, not as a truth to be forced on others, but as a truth to which one must witness.

The inner imperative of wisdom is that it is to be communicated to others rather than to be kept and savored for one's self. Matthew Fox, in his book *A Spirituality Named Compassion*,[6] claims that there are at least two models of spirituality. The first of these he refers to as "Climbing Jacob's Ladder," a model that emphasizes the solitary quest for enlightenment, a quest that tends to isolate the searcher and engages the person in a competitive struggle to be higher and better. Fox, however, sees another model, one he calls "Dancing Sarah's Circle." This model is a corporate venture which draws us into face-to-face, hand-to-hand relationship with others, a relationship in which celebration replaces climbing and in which interdependence replaces ruthless independence. Spirituality that draws men and women together in a sharing quest heightens their compassion, their sense of the oneness of men and women everywhere. The fruit of this spirituality is wisdom, a wisdom that incorporates the threefold movement of love: toward God, toward neighbor, toward one's self.

Notes

1. Guiseppe Verdi, *Ernani*, libretto by Francesco Maria Piave (based on Victor Hugo's *Hermani*), literal translation by William Weaver (New York: RCA, 1968).

2. Erik H. Erikson, *Childhood and Society* (New York: W. W. Norton, 1963), 274.

3. William Wordsworth, "The World is Too Much with Us."

4. *The Babylonian Talmud, Seder Mo'Ed*, vol. 4, translated under the editorship of Rabbi Dr. I. Epstein (London: Soncino Press, 1938).

5. Robert Penn Warren, *Flood* (New York: Random House, 1963), 239, 438.

6. Matthew Fox, *A Spirituality Named Compassion* (Minneapolis: Winston Press, 1979), 36-67.

Study Guide
The Gift of Wisdom

Reflection Questions

• Identify one or two persons whom you consider wise. With them in mind, answer these questions: What is wisdom? What does it mean to be wise? Write a definition and a list of qualities or characteristics that constitute wisdom for you.

• Which of the items in your list seem to fit you? Who else might they fit? How have you or they changed over the years? What can you learn from the "wisdom people" in your life that will help you become more wise?

Note: The Nigerian word for *older adults* translates into English with integrity as only "wisdom people." What a different way to think of them than is the norm in our society. In the Diocese of Tennessee, one congregation calls its older adult group "The Wisdom People."

• In the final stage of life we develop wisdom—"the wisdom of perceiving our lives as whole and with wholeness, despite the brokenness we share with all other persons." How can one experience wholeness in the midst of brokenness? Is that wholeness real or a denial of the reality of brokenness? Is it possible for younger people to experience that wholeness?

• Can one increase one's wisdom? If so, how?

• What is the value of wisdom in our society? How do we honor it? Dishonor it? What changes would you like to see that would increase our value for wisdom?

• Where have you experienced a sense of "owning" your life? What events in your life (or the lives of others) make you aware of a sense of owning nothing? At this point in your life, how do you balance the two?

- What gives you the feeling of independence? Of being alone? Are those the same thing? How are they connected? What helps you feel connected to others? Does that feel like interdependence? Dependence? What is the difference for you?

- Think of a loss that you have experienced, and that you would like to work with. (If you are in a group, make it one that you are willing to share.) What did you have to do to grieve that loss? Is there still unfinished work? What would help you to finish it? Have there been ways in which you feel the loss "redeemed and restored in God"? Do you know others who have had this experience?

- If God gave you the opportunity to make one request, what would you ask for?

Group Process

Purpose: To identify the characteristics of wisdom and reflect on their development to help people understand the potential for a unique wisdom achieved by embracing the challenges of old age.

Step 1:   Provide participants with paper and pencil. Ask them to think of one or two people whom they consider to be wise and make a list of the characteristics or qualities that lead them to identify them as wise.

Step 2:   Invite participants to share, in turn, one item from their lists not mentioned before until all items have been posted on the group's list. Discuss: Which of these qualities would be in **your** definition of wisdom? Why?

Step 3:   Ask participants to take 15 to 20 minutes to write a paragraph, poem, or song or to prepare artwork, dance, or a skit that expresses their idea about life's wholeness (provide paper, art supplies, quiet spaces). Invite participants to share what they have prepared.

Step 4:   Discuss: Are there common threads or themes that run
                     through all of the participants' representations? Are
                     there differences or singularities? Do any make a differ-
                     ence in the interpretation of your experiences? How do
                     they correlate with your listing of the characteristics
                     and qualities of wisdom?

Intergenerational Relationships: Adult Children and Aging Parents

Helen Kandel Hyman

The elderly do not live in a separate world of their own. Old age is not a sealed vacuum, impervious to outside influences. For better or for worse, the lives of the older generations are intertwined, often closely, with the lives of the younger generations. Like pebbles dropping into still waters, the fortunes—both good and bad—of older relatives send ripples down the years that touch and often strongly influence the lives of children, grandchildren, and even great-grandchildren. The younger generations send out ripples of their own, which in turn affect the lives of the older ones.

There is nothing new in this intergenerational involvement. It has been going on since the world began. Remember the story of Ruth and Naomi? The difference today is in scale—in numbers. In the past, few people lived to be old, so intergenerational relationships were fewer and lasted, with rare exceptions, for less time. Average life expectancy was 18 years in ancient Greece, 33 in the year 1600, and 47 when the twentieth century began. Today in the United States it is over 73. As Ronald Blythe points out in *A View from Winter*:

> If a Renaissance . . . man could return he would be as much astonished by the sight of two or three thousand septuagenarians and octogenarians lining a South Coast on a summer's day . . . as he would be by a television set. His was a world where it was the exception to go gray, to reach menopause, to become senile.

There are more than 29 million people over age 65 in the United States—more than 12% of the population. Predictions indicate that the elderly segment may rise to 25% at some point in the twenty-first century. By the year 2000 the older population is expected to reach 32 million. Earlier in this century few children grew to adulthood with living grandparents. Many of today's children will grow up knowing not only grandparents, but great-grandparents and even great-great-grandparents as well. Three and four-generation families are seen frequently, and the five-generation family is no longer uncommon. According to Dr. Robert Butler, former director of the National Institute on Aging, "This is the century not only of old age but of multigenerational families."

The family itself has undergone changes, particularly in the second half of this century. With the prevalence of divorce and remarriage, the family has enlarged its network with a proliferation of step-relationships. Today's children may have not only step-parents and step-siblings, but step-grandparents as well. So the ripples caused by elderly relatives are sending out ever-widening circles.

Until recently the involvement of families with their elderly members went unrecognized or unnoticed. As a matter of fact, the subject of old age in general was nearly taboo, especially in the period of the Youth Culture in the 1960s and 1970s. The emphasis then was on being young, acting young, feeling young. The families of the elderly struggled along for themselves when problems arose, trying to cope as best they could. Occasionally there was talk of the "nuclear" family— mother, father, children—living egocentric lives, exclusive, self-contained units sharing little and caring less about the older generations. This accusation was and still is justified for some families, but certainly not for the majority.

Gerontologists recognize that despite today's changing patterns the family plays a central role in the support system of its elderly relatives. Community services and programs, originally developed for the aging population, are now also designed to assist, extend, and relieve the ongoing care provided by younger family members. The old familiar accusation that "young people these days just don't care about their old parents" cannot be used broadside. More than three-quarters of the 29 million people over 65 have at least one living child. According to many surveys, aging parents and their children usually maintain ongoing contact with each other. Eighty-five percent of the parents with living children have at least one child living less than an hour away. Sixty-six percent saw one child the very day they were interviewed, and only 2% had not seen any of their children within the past year.

The family is acknowledged as playing a crucial role in the lives of its elderly members. When a husband becomes ill his wife usually acts as the primary care-giver—as he would act as hers—turning to children for backup support. When a parent is widowed or divorced, children then have to assume the primary role. Sons and daughters try to perform their roles well, yet many of them still feel that they are not doing enough. As hard as they try, they still feel guilty about the perceived inadequacy of their efforts, suffering periodic unease that "we are not caring enough for those who cared for us." The classic guilt-raiser "One mother can take care of 10 children but 10 children cannot take care of one old mother" strikes home to many. The younger generation, trying to juggle a variety of conflicting responsibilities, may even feel that King Lear was pointing directly to them when he wailed, "How sharper than a serpent's tooth it is to have a thankless child!"

Who are all these "thankless children?" They are the middle generations sandwiched between the older and the younger, pulled in opposing directions by stresses on either side. They are found in every part of the country and at every economic level. Some of them are young parents rearing young children, building careers, and at the same time trying not to neglect their aging parents. "Do I get the sitter for the children so I can be with father? Or do I get the sitter for father so I can be with the children?" sighs a young mother. "Can I accept a promotion a thousand miles away? If I do, I'll be leaving my old parents behind. How will they manage? But what about my own career?" worries a young father.

Another group of "thankless children" are in their 40s and 50s. They have no youngsters around anymore and fewer domestic responsibilities. Life should be easier for them by now, but perhaps it is not. Perhaps they are facing the high cost of college tuition for their adolescent children and working harder to pay the bills. Perhaps they are at peak career with demanding jobs or—conversely—experiencing career setbacks, lack of advancement, financial reverses, even unemployment or layoffs. Perhaps the women are now back to work again—and enjoying it—after years of domestic routine. Perhaps husbands and wives are seeing their own old age coming closer or experiencing some of the diffuse, bewildering symptoms of menopause, male and female.

And then there is a third group—men and women in their 60s and 70s, still concerned about parents in their 80s and 90s, and even over

100. (When baby-boomers graduate to senior status, projections suggest, there will be more than one million centenarians. If this projection comes true, there should be several million sons and daughters, probably 80-ish themselves, still calling someone Mom or Dad.) These older sons and daughters are already in the senior class themselves, many of them grandparents by now. They are looking squarely at their own aging, perhaps with diminished health, stamina, and resources. They may be coping with their own retirement and reduced incomes. They may even be widowed by now. What if their children and their grandchildren still need help? How can there be enough physical, financial, or emotional strength to go around, to share with other family members equally?

There is more help for these middle generations today than there was a few decades ago. Starting in the 1970s, old age, once taboo, became quite a favored subject in the popular media. The public has become more familiar with the variety of supportive services available in many communities. Instead of trying to solve all their problems themselves, people have discovered there is help to be found when elderly relatives develop problems. Nonprofessional people can often talk quite knowledgeably about nursing homes, day-care centers, Meals on Wheels, transportation services, Social Security, Medicare and Medicaid.

More professionals are being trained every year. The field of gerontology is one of the fastest-growing career opportunities in the United States. *The New York Times* reported in 1988 that 900 programs in gerontology were being offered in 400 educational institutions—universities, colleges, and junior colleges.

Even with such community services available, many families are still reluctant to turn to them, feeling that if they do they will be breaking the commandment to "honor your father and your mother."

"If I let someone else help my parents, it will look as though I don't love them enough," one such reluctant daughter may say. Or, "People will think I'm not a good daughter." Why should this be true? Is love simply chauffeuring and housecleaning and cooking and nursing? Often it is harder for children to show their love when they let themselves become overburdened with extra responsibilities. An aging mother might discover that if outsiders help with her domestic routines there will be more time for pleasure and real companionship with her children. Perhaps she'll have a chance to talk more about her feelings, worries, and fears, and perhaps her children will be freer to listen.

When families are willing to ask for outside help, they may find to their dismay that not much exists in their communities or that it is prohibitively expensive. Too little is reimbursable under Medicare or not enough is allowed by Medicaid. (As of 1994, the whole future of health care and health reform for all ages—the elderly included—is unclear.) If outside services do exist, one person is needed to act as general coordinator, making sure that the help an elderly parent needs flows constantly and does not break down. This caretaker role has been traditionally taken by daughters, most frequently by one particular daughter. She either assumes the role voluntarily or is assigned it by her parents or brothers and sisters. When there is no daughter to act as caretaker, especially when extensive or intensive care is needed, nursing home placement may become necessary. The daughter's role in the care of the elderly is considered so crucial that one gerontologist claims that the phrase "alternatives to institutionalization" is merely a euphemism for the word "daughters." Sometimes these daughters are over 65 themselves.

In any discussion of relationships between older and younger generations, there is always the danger that problems will be emphasized and benefits ignored. Tolstoy wrote in *Anna Karenina*, "Happy families are all alike; every unhappy family is unhappy in its own way." There is a tendency to focus on the various "ways" of difficulties that arise for the elderly and affect their families. But the benefits derived from warm intergenerational relationships must never be ignored. They are unique in our experience of life and may offer treasures to be found nowhere else.

That parents and grandparents are growing older does not necessarily mean that they will ever turn to their families for anything except companionship and pleasure. Millions of older people continue right on into their 70s and 80s—even into their 90s—firmly in control of their own lives and often still firmly controlling their children's lives, too. They may still pursue their own interests and routines, handle their own finances, make their own decisions, and probably resent interference. Old age of itself is not a problem, nor does it inevitably produce problems or dependency.

Countless stories can be told of gratifying relationships between the generations with love and mutual enjoyment, as well as concrete help, flowing as much from the older to the younger as from the younger to the older. The generations mix and mingle, each one living independently but drawing strength and support from the other. Vigorous, independent, self-sufficient octogenarians are not only splendid sources of enjoyment, wisdom, and advice for their children and grandchildren, but they can be comforting role models as well. Their very satisfactory existence can prove to younger people that growing old is not so terrible after all. Old age and the aging process are still shrouded in misconceptions and false assumptions. No wonder men and women approach their own aging with fear and dread.

Look at the most familiar misconceptions that are widely held: To be old is to be sick, lonely, poor, useless, finished, sexless. These descriptions do fit some of the nation's elderly, but they can be applied to many younger people, too. They certainly cannot be applied to all the elderly. Every day millions are proving these myths false by continuing to function productively right to the end. The myth that to be old is to be sick can be refuted by fact and figure. Of the more than 24 million elderly, only 15% are unable to carry on normal activities. The elderly population average less than 15 days a year in bed because of illness. And, finally, for those who believe that old people usually end up in nursing homes, only 5% of the elderly are in institutions at any one time.

One of the most serious causes of misunderstanding is that catchall phrase "65 and older," which is used to describe senior citizens. More and more people are living into the later decades. Our total population has increased threefold since 1900, but the elderly segment has increased fivefold. The group over 85 is the fastest-growing segment of the population. So when we blithely talk of the nation's senior citizens, we may be talking of a range of 30 years. A daughter of 72 may be caring for a mother of 95, yet both these women are included in that crude category.

The 65th birthday is not a magical date when people plunge headlong into old age as into a swimming pool. Yet this label is placed on 29 million individuals who have an infinite variety of individual interests, life-styles, personalities, problems, and physical ailments. There are the sick and the healthy, the introverts and the extroverts, the productive and the inactive, the joiners and the loners, just as there are at any other stage in the life cycle. People over 65 are eligible for Medicare or Medicaid; they can draw pensions and collect Social Security. But these are the only things they all have in common with each other.

Look at the first three decades of life and the changes that 30 years can bring. Clear stages are recognized: infancy, childhood, adolescence, maturity. But the last 30 years are lumped together in a single category. Professionals are trying to make more sense out of these years by referring to the young-old—65 to 74, the middle-aged old—75 to 84, and the old-old—85 and up. Health problems and needs are different for each of these stages. A condition that is an inconvenience for someone who is young-old may become a difficult disability for the same person at middle-aged old and possibly an incapacitating problem at the old-old stage. For example, poor vision may one day turn into blindness, diabetes may progress until amputation is necessary, arthritis may become totally crippling.

It is unfair, however, to be too critical of the fact that the final 30 years have not been more realistically described. These years are confusing because the aging process is so unpredictable. It moves at different rates for different people. It is known within a certain range when children will walk, talk, go through puberty. But there is no such predictability in the aging process, even for brothers and sisters in the same family. Every individual suffers a certain amount of physical loss as the years go by. This goes on visibly, as skin and hair change, and invisibly within the body. But there is no predicting when these losses will take place or when, if ever, the losses will become serious problems. The recuperative powers of two patients of the same age recovering from the same serious illness can vary tremendously. One may return to autonomous living in a matter of weeks while the other retires into permanent invalidism. For this reason it is difficult for the families and for the elderly themselves to see into the future and to figure out how much care will be needed and for how long. Personality and emotions play a crucial role, too, complicating things even further.

Frank Wilson and his younger sister, Mary, were both in their 80s, and both suffered from seriously impaired vision. Frank, a determined and indomitable character, managed somehow despite his semiblindness to live alone, take care of himself, even to travel. He read the newspaper every day with a complicated contraption he had rigged up for himself consisting of a green eyeshade, a high intensity light, and a rolled-up tube of paper through which he focused with one eye on the print. His sister, with the same degree of impairment and several years younger, gave up before she was 80, referred to herself as blind, and became completely dependent on her overburdened younger daughter.

Another prevailing false assumption is that independence is an all-or-nothing situation for the elderly. When widowed Gilbert Cuseo had a stroke in his mid-70s, his children were frantic while he was recuperating in the hospital. "Father can't live alone any more. He'll have to go to a nursing home or come to live with one of us. But which one of us can take him?" Luckily his children were in such a turmoil that they were unable to make any decision. In the meantime Mr. Cuseo surprised everyone by making an almost complete recovery. Families often assume the worst and see nothing but disaster ahead when an aging parent suffers a stroke or a heart attack, or when doctors discover dreaded symptoms of cancer, glaucoma, or diabetes. But such panic is often premature. The road to the nursing home is a long one with many detours and stopovers along the way. Remember that at any given time only 5% of the elderly are in nursing homes. And contrary to what many sons and daughters assume, most parents do not want to live with their children but prefer to remain independent as long as possible—ideally, forever.

Even if total independence cannot continue forever, some portion of it can usually be maintained. Except in sudden tragic instances—a massive stroke, a major heart attack, a serious accident—people do not usually go from total independence to total dependence overnight. Independence usually dwindles slowly away.

After an acute illness or with the slow progression of a chronic physical condition, an elderly man may lose some portion of his ability to manage independently. He may need help in that area of his life which has become weak, but he may be as strong as ever in other areas. If he can find the necessary support, he may still be able to continue living independently. "A good daughter is the one who takes care of her aging father" may have once been considered a fine definition of filial devotion. But a better definition today might be "A good daughter is the one who helps her aging father take care of himself."

Care for the elderly may be described as having three levels of intensity. The lowest level can be called *on-and-off care*. It is not continual and not intense. Help may be needed only during special periods related to a minor illness, a depressive episode, recovery from a fall. Temporary care of this kind may be especially supportive following a bereavement, the death of a husband, a wife, a child. It is also essential during a posthospital convalescence.

Eighty-seven-year-old Sandra Rose, who lived alone in an apartment complex for the elderly, recently had a double cataract operation. After a brief hospital stay she returned to her own apartment and was willing to have a homemaker, hired by her daughter, come in four hours a day. But as she told her daughter soon afterwards "I get my new glasses on Thursday and then, thank God, that woman goes!" Once she felt able to manage alone she was impatient to have her on-and-off care turned off for good—or at least until she needed it again.

Ongoing supportive care is a middle-range level of care needed by older people whose disabilities have permanently limited their functioning in some areas but not in others. They are not likely to improve, but they are able to get along well enough if they have continuing support in their weak areas. Supportive ongoing care may be required by older people who are severely arthritic, partially blind, or partially paralyzed, as well as by those who have no special infirmity but are generally weakening. It is also needed by those who are physically sound but mentally impaired.

Finally, there is *long-term intensive care* for the chronically and seriously ill or disabled. It is only at this point that independence finally dwindles away. This level of care is the most demanding, the most difficult to provide, and the most disastrously expensive. All three levels of care can be provided by a support system of relatives, friends, and community services; however, when long-term intensive care becomes too burdensome, nursing home placement may be the only solution.

The independence so treasured by the elderly can be jeopardized by devoted children even when there are no crises requiring some level of care. Mindful of the commandment to "honor your father and your mother," and anxious to see themselves or to be seen by others as "good children," some sons and daughters may never realize that too much caring can be as harmful as too little. A daughter who rushes in at the first sign of faltering to "take over" for dear old Mom and Dad may seem to show admirable filial devotion. She may never dream that this devotion may weaken still further the old couple's faltering sense of self-reliance and self-esteem, making them become prematurely dependent. When children assume too much responsibility and make unilateral decisions according to their own rather than their parents' wishes, they become benign dictators. Such children would be surprised to learn that they may actually be killing their parents with kindness.

Kindness and devotion are sterling qualities. Many an elderly man or woman would welcome a small amount of both, but these qualities are more likely to produce successful results when accompanied by a genuine understanding of each individual's wishes, personality, and preferred life-style. The efforts of well-meaning children to provide "the kind of life we want for Mom and Dad" would probably succeed better if they encouraged instead "the kind of life Mom and Dad want for *themselves*." Look at these examples of benign dictatorship:

- Forcing Dad to retire because of his heart condition, to take it easy and enjoy himself at last. To some fathers, retirement is tantamount to dying.

- Taking Mom from the run-down, dangerous urban neighborhood where she has lived for 50 years to the security and comfort of a pleasant suburb. Her family may feel greatly relieved that she is finally safe, but the alien surroundings may trigger a severe depression in a bewildered, confused Mom.

- Repeatedly reassuring Mom and Dad with the statement, "You must relax. We'll take care of everything." Everything may include driving the car, cooking meals, planning a vacation, choosing a doctor, making decisions. Such kind reassurance can boomerang. The message Mom and Dad receive is that they are no longer capable of taking care of anything.

The most successful decisions are likely to be those arrived at jointly by everyone, with the elderly stating their preferences and the young offering suggestions and warnings.

Shortly after Katherine Prazer was widowed at 79, she announced that she was putting her house on the market and moving from

Ohio to Florida to be near her old friend, Jenny. Her children knew that she and their father had been contemplating this move before he died, but they were worried that she was taking such a radical step alone and too quickly after she was widowed. They understood why she needed to get away from the old house so full of memories and didn't try to dissuade her. But they did suggest a compromise plan and urged her to make a temporary rather than a permanent move. "Why not rent the house for a year and see how things go in Florida?" her son suggested. "You may not like it there." Her daughter added, "You may not even like Jenny." Katherine accepted the compromise and took off for Florida. Exactly a year later she was ready to move back into her old house. "Jenny's a bore!" she announced to her children. "All she does is talk about her health. And anyway, who wants to live in a place where it never snows?"

No discussion of intergenerational relationships can be complete without some reference to emotions, not only the feelings of the older and younger generations toward each other, but also feelings of younger people about old age in general and their parents' aging specifically. These feelings may seriously affect how they behave toward their parents. Those with a positive attitude toward growing old are more likely to be able to reach out to their elderly parents with concern and constructive support. But if old age is viewed with apprehension and dread—as it is by so many in today's society—a parent's aging can be very threatening. It forces younger people to contemplate their own old age and eventual death.

Feelings also intervene as families watch valued relatives, formerly sources of strength and comfort, begin to decline. A mother's hands shake. A father becomes forgetful or slightly disoriented. These well-loved people no longer can provide the support they once did. Such changes are painful to see, but some children can accept them— although with great sadness and regret—realizing that their parents will not live forever. Others cannot contemplate losing the people they have always depended on and may react with fear or even anger. Or they may refuse to admit that anything is wrong, ignoring physical symptoms and complaints. A problem may be denied until it is too late for medical intervention that might alleviate or perhaps even reverse the frightening symptoms.

Perhaps the most crucial emotions are the tangled, mixed-up feelings between the generations. Here again, when emotions are positive, it is easier for children to remain close to their parents and to be supportive when needed. When feelings are negative or conflicted, problems between the generations are likely to intensify.

Long-standing relationships between parents and children often determine how much contact there will be in later years and how much these children are willing or able to help when their parents grow old. These relationships have been 30, 40, 50 years in the making. Some relationships modify, and the intensity may lessen when children grow up and move away from daily parental involvement; but lifetime patterns are not easy to change. One daughter asks her widowed father to live with her and her family. Together they form a successful three-generation household. Her neighbor down the street cannot take this step. She loves her father, too, but differently. Her love is mixed with fear, or with a dependency he'd never let her outgrow, or with resentment that her older sister always was, and still is, his favorite. The way he treated her as a child may well determine how she is able to treat him when she is grown up and he is old. But the guilt she feels because she cannot do more for him can trigger another emotion, anger. She is angry with herself for not helping more and angry at him for making her feel guilty. She withdraws even further and when others provide whatever help is needed, feels guiltier yet.

Feelings also intervene when brothers and sisters try to work cooperatively with each other to provide the help their parents need. While these cooperative efforts produce wonders in some families, in others where there has always been tension and rivalry, these emotions are likely to flare up again and torpedo the best-laid plans. Brothers and sisters often do not agree on a course to be followed, so a stalemate occurs. The ailing mother or father is forgotten while old battles dating from the nursery are waged all over again. The favorite child and the less favored may keep on fighting for the prize "Mother loves me best," even when the children are in their 60s and Mother is over 80. Mother may still fan the flames and play favorites from her wheelchair.

Some adults can face up to their feelings about their parents, or their brothers and sisters, and evaluate them honestly. Others are unaware of what they feel or, if aware, deny it to themselves and everyone else. An objective observer, a doctor, a minister, or a family therapist can often help family members sort out all these mixed-up feelings and learn to live with them. But strangely, even though they are in painful turmoil, many families seek out this kind of help only as a last resort. They may doggedly keep right on searching for the right nursing home, the right housing, the right homemaker, the right doctor—never realizing that their tangled emotions are preventing them from finding the right anything. When these emotions are faced honestly, they no longer get in the way of constructive action, and both generations are better off.

The commandment to "honor your father and your mother" does not offer specific guidelines as to how the honor should be provided. This is just as well, as no one pat formula can be applied. When it comes to intergenerational relationships, the personality and life-style of every close family member have to be taken into account. So do finances, job pressures, and health factors. Solutions that work for one family may not work for another and should probably not even be considered. As one young woman said recently, "I can't have Mother live with us. It just won't work. But we all want to help her and we are helping. Life's pretty good now for all of us—for Mother, my children, and for my husband and me. It's not perfect, but I don't really expect there is a perfect solution."

It would be comforting to most daughters and sons if they could have such realistic expectations. Then perhaps they would feel less guilt when things are imperfect. No matter how hard she tries, a daughter will never be able to make her parents young again. She may not even be able to make them happy again. She's never going to turn them back into the strong, supportive people they used to be. She's certainly not going to transform them into the parents she always wished she had—but never did. But if she sets her goals realistically, she can expect to find ways to make her parents' lives easier, more meaningful, more satisfying, less lonely, and generally more livable, without demanding too many sacrifices from her children, her husband, and herself. If she can accomplish this, then she and her parents will have more time to enjoy each other's company before it's too late.

Study Guide

Intergenerational Relationships:
Adult Children and Aging Parents

Reflection Questions

• In preparation for writing a dialogue with an older person who has been an influence in your life, begin by listing the "stepping stones" in that person's life—his or her most important benchmarks (as well as you can surmise them). Limit yourself to 6 to 12 stepping stones.

• Next write a "focus statement"—a paragraph or so that explains why you would like to have the dialogue. (It may be that you have unfinished business with the person, that you would like to learn some of his or her wisdom, that there is something you would like to say to this person, or that you have some other agenda.)

• Write the dialogue. Start with yourself, putting "me" in the left margin. Write until you come to a pause. Then write the other person's name in the left margin and what he or she has to say. Continue until you feel it is finished.

There is no wrong way to do this. Whatever comes out is fine. You might do it differently another time; that is fine, too.

• When you have finished the dialogue, take a few minutes to relax and see what feelings you are experiencing. Then reread the dialogue, and see what it evokes. You may continue in dialogue with this person, or others, at another time.

[This design is adapted from the work of Ira Progoff. For more on the use of the dialogue (and journaling in general), see his *At a Journal Workshop*, New York: Dialogue House, 1975.]

Group Process

This group might be either intergenerational or unigenerational. A leader who can encourage discussion and out common threads from the discussion is essential.

Step 1:   Have participants spend a few seconds in silence so that all members can have time to remember an older relative who has had a significant impact on their life. This may be a positive impact, a negative impact, or a mixed impact. (If a participant hasn't been lucky enough to have a relative who qualifies, he or she may think of another older person who has been an influence.)

Step 2:   Ask each member to identify the special person and to say a few words about the impact the older adult had on his or her life. (If the group is too large to get feedback from each member, divide into pairs or small groups and have them share.)

Step 3:   Elicit from the group and record on newsprint: What were the rewards of that relationship (or of other relationships with older adults)?

If participants have problems with this question, you may make suggestions to see if they experienced the following rewards:

• Elders gave a sense of history and roots.

• Elders' first-hand experiences brought to life the participants' academic study of those times.

• Elders provided a model for their own aging.

• Elders taught skills such as knitting, writing, how to look at things on vacation, how to have fun.

• Older people gave participants a sense of their own value: "they were not too busy for me"; "I felt cherished."

• Elders appreciated things participants made or did in a way other adults didn't.

Point out that most of what we initially think of when we talk about care-giving relationships is the burden and problem, yet we should look at the gifts that have been identified.

Step 4: Record on newsprint: What were the problems? If not listed, here are some problems commonly found that may be added:

- Legal and financial issues—Wills, durable powers of attorney, limited powers of attorney, guardianship, trusts, record keeping, planning for "shortfalls."

- Health issues—Including concern about change in living arrangements.

- Ignorance of community services—Share information on available social services. If you need assistance, contact the agency on aging in your community.

- Emotional issues—Guilt, resentment, anger, fear, love, sadness, confusion, ambivalence, hopelessness, uncertainty.

Point out that such issues are *normal,* not pathological, and that acknowledging them can be helpful in itself.

Step 5: Record on newsprint answers to the following question: What can the congregation do?

If not listed, include: education, support of care-givers (individually or in groups), transportation, emergency meals, information and referral, Stephen Ministries, or other lay pastoral care training.

Step 6: Next steps: Explore with the group what they would like to do next to utilize what it has discovered. Depending on the group, you might focus on individual goals (e.g., calling the area agency on aging for help with one participant's mother's transportation problems) or on group goals (e.g., starting a care-giver support group in a congregation).

The Church as Family

JoAnn S. Jamann-Riley

St. Paul instructed the members of the early church on their special function, as the church, to serve one another as family. "For as in one body we have many members, and not all the members have the same function, so we, who are many, are one body in Christ, and individually we are members one of another" (Rom. 12:4-5).

To Jesus, the church family was defined as those who do the will of God (Mark 3:35). According to John Westerhoff, "Jesus consistently denied primary obligations to his cultural family and committed himself unreservedly to his 'faith family.'"[1]

Following this mandate, the church evolved to bring others into the body, to feed their needs and to send them forth to continue in this pattern. Historically, the church family has been and continues to be intergenerational and inclusive, welcoming all the followers of Christ irrespective of culture, race, gender, health, and age.

The church, or faith family, for centuries also functioned as a social and "social welfare" system. As society changed in the United States, some of these traditional church functions became subsumed by the development of community agencies. The late 1990s and the first several decades of the twenty-first century will see a resurgence of the importance of the church's role in society based on Jesus' faith family model. This is because present and projected demographic and societal changes include not only a reconfiguration of the population into a more even spread of age groups, but also more widespread geographic living patterns of biological families, increased mobility of individuals over the life span, and shifting values and resources.

The need for the church family to resume its former role of care-giver, advocate, and intervener is increasingly important in today's society, based on the demographic changes and recent advances in technology. The church must also assume a role in addressing and clarifying changing life values.

Every church needs to assess and evaluate the specific needs of its church family and community. Individual and/or internal family changes need to be assessed, for life changes often create stress that can affect a person's health and well-being. How people are coping with their emergencies, as well as with their long-term changes such as widowhood, are appropriate areas for local churches to assess. Various relationships should be reviewed for type of interaction, frequency, and quality of contact. As a result of such an assessment, one church organized a contact network to render immediate assistance in emergencies. Another church established an adult day care center.

As part of the church's assessment, it is necessary to evaluate what is available through and needed by the community. Meals-on-Wheels or Dial Transport are ecumenical activities that address community needs through outreach. If we view our communities as all God's children, then our faith communities will grow and develop. Interdenominational and interfaith programming and services best exemplify how each local church is the body (family), just as the universal church is Christ's body. "Now you are the body of Christ and individually members of it" (1 Cor. 12:27).

Characteristics of the Healthy Church Family

The interdependent connections of the church family usually start as a casual network of friends and acquaintances. As life goes on, the bonds of friendship intertwine, and grow deeper, and the realization emerges that the interconnectedness is important to their very being. The fullness of a member's life has become dependent on the fullness of the other members' lives. The church family has truly become responsible for itself. Thus the healthy church family develops.

Some of the healthy family characteristics identified by Dolores Curran may be distilled to describe traits of a healthy church family: shared religious core, sense of belonging, shared responsibility, value mutual service, and active problem solving.[2]

Religious Core—A shared religious core is the very foundation of the church family. Common beliefs are the center of individual and family spirituality. The steadiness of shared beliefs and practices draws the members of the family closer together and gives them the anchor required to reach out to others in the world around them. Open exploration of the shared faith empowers each member of the family to grow in wisdom and grace. Complementing corporate worship are small worship groups, study groups, and servant groups. The shared religious core enhances opportunities to pray and praise together. The solid foundation of a shared religious core in the church family enables each member to express God's presence in his or her life.

Belonging and Shared Responsibility—Sharing a deep religious core gives each member of the church family a sense of belonging. There is a kinship based on scriptural knowledge and understanding, rich religious traditions, and desires to share the joy and peace of the religious experience. As the church family matures, it develops traditions and rituals that are particularly meaningful for promoting the spirituality of the family.

The expression of commitment comes from shared responsibility based on mutual respect and acceptance of individual differences. The members develop a sense of trust in each other, which gives an inner certainty that actions are based on goodwill, done in a timely fashion, and communicated truthfully. Thus at one time or another every member of the church family is a giver and receiver.

Value Mutual Service—In the healthy church family there is no busy-work. The contributions of each member are truly valued. Sharing leisure time, for example, gives each member a chance to know each other better or gives some members a chance to reduce their stress levels. Indeed, such informal times often serve to increase our sense of playfulness, excitement, and good humor, all of which benefit the group. Frequently, I have found it difficult to get older people to accept the services of others. It may be hard to realize that receiving is often a gift of giving as well. Simply, one cannot have the pleasure and joy of giving if there is no one to receive the gift or service. Thus, in the healthy church family, high value is placed on mutual service.

Active Problem Solving—As with any family, there will be problems within the church family. However, the healthy family admits its problems and seeks solutions. Truthful, open communications about perceived problems will offend no one and will recognize the valuable contributions of everyone. Church families will experience the problems of changing membership and resources, societal and environmental changes, and the monotony of routine practices.

The healthy church family will not be satisfied simply to identify its problems. It will seek solutions that enhance the growth and development of each of its members. The search for solutions begins with individual and group prayer—requesting guidance. It is not easy to discern the direction and actions the individual or group must take to nourish the soul as well as the psychosocial-biological being of each person of the family as a group.

Problems within the church family are inevitable, but with the addressing of problems and the finding of solutions comes strength. The family ties become more numerous, stronger, and intertwined. It is hard to accept the imperfections in ourselves and others, but with God's help the church can help us to have a sense of family. The church family can help each of us to care for others and to reach beyond ourselves.

The Healthy Church Family in Action

The activities within a church family reflect its "state of health." In other words, if the characteristics of a healthy church family are known and felt by its members, the existing activities strengthen the church family. In returning to the list of these characteristics—shared religious core, sense of belonging, shared responsibility, value mutual service, and active problem solving—we can recognize that activities are not merely a series of programs, but a series of gifts to each other: love, support, and togetherness. There is not an expectation of receiving gifts; rather, there is a slow growth of caring and support. These caring relationships grow within the context of many different church-sponsored activities. It is the spirit of those who enter into the activities that brings the quality of family life to the activities, not the activities themselves.

Impact on Lives

The church family has a unique contribution to make in the life of any one person. It does not replace biological or cultural families. It does not supply resources better given by diverse community agencies. It does not supplant individual initiative or neighborhood friends. Rather, the church family meets needs to enhance the quality of an individual's life and integrates that person into a loving circle of friends. These friends offer a perpetual interaction and human support found in family relationships.

The following two stories are told for better understanding of the tremendous impact the church has on the quality of our lives. Notice the similarities in these stories—commitment and unconditional sharing and caring.

As we grow older our circle of relatives and friends continues to shrink if we do not make new friends and "adopt new relatives." Church families have potential for constant change. For example, Mary had many friends, an active career in teaching, and a small biological family. After her husband died she moved to a retirement community in South Carolina, where she remained involved in community and church activities. Now she is 85 years old and has no living relatives. Her longtime friends live hundreds of miles away, so they visit only by telephone or letters. Sometimes this is difficult for Mary because her eyesight is failing and her financial resources are limited. Also, Mary is fiercely independent. Nonetheless, she nurtures and sustains a strong church family.

Mary and her church family have a beautiful interdependence. Mary graciously helps to maintain a prayer chain within her church by initiating the calls. When there is a special need, there is never any question that Mary is available and willing to start the telephone calls. Her young friends, preschoolers, look forward to the timely cards she sends to them at Sunday school. When possible, Mary accepts transportation from one of her church family to attend the prayer and healing service, thereby contributing to the corporate worship, as well as to offer herself as a prayer intercessor. To assist Mary in her everyday life, her church brothers and sisters call or visit her frequently, accept the responsibility to help her maintain her independence by living in her own home, and give her the assurance that her instructions will be followed when she dies. Mary's life is as full as she wants it to be, and her church family is blessed by her warm and tender caring and sharing.

Another example demonstrates how a strong church family can affect one person over most of his or her life span. Tom assumed the responsibilities as sexton at an Episcopal church in a northwestern state when he was approximately 30 years of age. He was developmentally disabled by meningitis when he was a boy. Following this illness he also suffered seizures that continued throughout his lifetime. He never married, and his parents and siblings preceded him in death. Tom lived most of his life a block from the church and spent the bulk of his time working around the grounds and buildings of the church. He retired after 34 years of service as sexton. Although his health continued to fail after his retirement, he was able to live in his little house near the church until his death at 71 because of the love and care of his church family and the resources of the community they garnered on his behalf.

Specific Activities

There are specific activities within the church that can foster and sustain the qualities of family life, for example, the child-grandparent activities being established in many churches. These programs bring together young people who need the consistent love and attention of an older individual. "Adoptive grandparents" may tutor children after school, just be there for chats, or expand the children's world through reading to them or taking them on short trips within the community. In other programs the child may assist the older person by doing errands, light work around the home, or daily telephoning to assure the security of the older person. The variations of this theme are limitless. What really matters is the identification of a *real* need and the willingness of all generations to participate. These programs can easily reach beyond a single church's congregation.

Another activity that nurtures and strengthens families is the interfaith InHome Respite Care Service in Bethlehem, Pennsylvania. A small group of individuals recognized that the great need for in-home respite care was not going to be met by social agencies. After prayerful consideration, several persons launched a program to link trained volunteers with caretakers who needed some brief, consistent relief. This program has grown and developed to include various congregations that are meeting the needs of scores of care-givers. These care-givers may or may not be members of the churches from which the respite volunteers are drawn. Programmed relationships are generally more limited and more formalized than that of Mary and her church family. Nevertheless, the bonds established in the respite care triads (care receiver—care-giver—respite care volunteer) exemplify the commitment and unconditional love of the church family in action.

Another constellation of church members that encourages the establishment and growth of church families is composed of adult groups. They are formed around specific needs, such as those of single individuals living alone who require socialization with other adults. The groups may plan and participate in worship, community service, fellowship activities, or any combination thereof. Bonds within groups of this type often grow very strong over the years.

Illustrative of the depth of some of these adult church family relationships were the "prayer sisters" I encountered in my home health practice. Ruth and Betty were too ill to be able to leave their homes. Nonetheless, they were a constant source of strength to each other through prayer and telephone sharing. It was not uncommon for them to call each other in the middle of the night when one of them needed spiritual comfort or guidance. What a beautiful caring and sharing relationship they had with each other. What a beautiful example they were to others!

Another adult group that has been a great pleasure to observe is a Men's Churchyard Team. Their stated purpose is to keep the church grounds neat, clean, and beautiful. The greatest benefit of the group is the fellowship it fosters and the family bonds it has established. New members have included some women who also enjoy the yard work, but the relationships have grown beyond the task. The members are there for each other when one of them needs assistance. The joy they share with one another has enabled them to reach beyond their group to initiating broader fellowship such as an annual oyster roast plus many more activities.

True family life is basic to the human condition. Some activities may work for some churches and not for others. The activity itself is not important. What is important is that the activity have a meaningful core to establish a group and that there be opportunities for members of the group to form bonds with each other. Meeting regularly enables people to learn to know each other and to get beyond past roles or expectations. To begin with, small groups are generally more successful in initiating family bonds because there is more opportunity for consistent sharing. The members may come together to pray, to have dinner, or to take on a special task, but often they find that they are sharing more of themselves than they expected. This is the beginning of the interdependent connections of church family life.

It is important to emphasize that the continued health of the church family demands the participation of all of its members. John Westerhoff points this out in his book, *Living the Faith Community*: ". . . a living Christian faith demands a community of faith that shares a common story, authority, worship, and life—a community of faith engaging intentionally in those processes that best help its faith to become conscious, living, and active in the personal and corporate lives of its people."[3]

Like good stewards of the manifold grace of God, serve one another with whatever gift each of you has received. Whoever speaks must do so as one speaking the very words of God; whoever serves must do so with the strength that God supplies, so that God may be glorified in all things through Jesus Christ (1 Peter 4:10-11).

Notes

1.   John H. Westerhoff, *Living the Faith Community: The Church That Makes a Difference* (Minneapolis: Winston Press; San Francisco: Harper & Row, 1985), 2.

2.   Dolores Curran, *Traits of a Healthy Family: Fifteen Traits Commonly Found in Healthy Families by Those Who Work with Them* (Minneapolis: Winston Press, 1983).

3.   John H. Westerhoff, *Living the Faith Community*, 106.

Study Guide
The Church as Family

Reflection Questions

• Take two sheets of paper. Write "My Family" (however you define it) on one sheet and "My Church Family" on the other. Draw a line down the center of each sheet and label the left column "Stresses" and the right column "Hopes." Fill in the stresses and hopes you can identify for your two families. Review what you have written. What does it tell you about the needs and the opportunities in each family situation?

• Consider the times in your life when you needed family other than your biological kin. How did (or could) the church meet your needs? If you could speak to the members of your congregation now, what would you ask or tell them?

• Does this reflection give you ideas about ways in which you might be family to others in your congregation who might be in need of familylike support?

• Look at Curran's five characteristics of a healthy church family. Which seem to fit your congregation? Which do not? How can you help move your congregation toward greater health?

Group Process

Step 1:   Discuss "What is a family?" and record your answers on newsprint.

Step 2:   Discuss "How well does the church fit the characteristics you have identified as being familial?" How do the members of your group feel about this fit or lack of fit? Should the church be like a family? What might be the disadvantages of being like a family? The advantages?

Step 3: Brainstorm the following: If there are older adults who are members of your congregation, and who need more family than is present for them, how might your congregation be family for them? Think of as many ideas as you can, without judging them.

Step 4: Carefully consider the ideas you have generated. Which ones might work in your own setting? Who might have a special call to implement them? Come up with a tentative game plan for the ideas you think are best.

Step 5: Make a specific plan, with all the steps you can think of, and a time line for implementing your plan. (Consider letting the Episcopal Society for Ministry on Aging know about your work, so that it can be shared with others. Call or write: 323 Wyandotte Street, Bethlehem, PA 18015-1527; 610-868-5400.)

Toward Creative Aging:
The Church's Response

Karen Johnson Karner

At present, regardless of your age, you may still believe that you are quite a distance from "old age." Perhaps you may have only recently begun to think about aging as it applies to you. You are not alone, for many of us are uncomfortable in thinking about aging. With the gift of added years comes the fear of physical and intellectual decline.

Our society encourages us to continue to deny our own aging, by emphasizing the advantages of youth. Advertisements, entertainments, our entire societal structure implies that every person should try to stay young as long as possible. We use humor to soften the blow. For example, heard recently at a 40th birthday celebration, "It's better to be over the hill than under it!" We learn that youth is "good" and old age is "bad." So when we talk about aging, there's a tendency to refer to "them" when, in reality, "they" are "us." This pessimistic view about our own aging affects how we relate to people older than ourselves, with a tendency to focus on disabilities rather than abilities and the potential for growth. As citizens, our votes on issues that affect older people, such as health care, housing, and transportation, are influenced by our attitudes toward aging. As church members, our various ministries can be influenced by our personal views of aging. And, most important, our personal views of aging direct the course of our own lives—for we are likely to live up to our expectations, be they negative or positive.

The church is the social institution with the greatest potential for reaching us in our later years. Typically 40 to 60% of congregations are composed of retired persons.[1] Certainly, the church has responded to the needs of its older members. However, its ministry has often been concerned with their social welfare, while not directly addressing their need for learning and spiritual growth. The church has addressed visible needs such as transportation, food, and social services. This "social welfare" approach to the ministry on aging labels the older members of the congregation as dependent and in need of services. And this emphasis on such social and physical issues is also reflected in educational programming. Despite the increasing proportion of older adults in most congregations, educational programming continues to address its younger members. Furthermore, existing educational activities for older adults often focus on the problems of aging, paying little attention to the opportunities of aging.

The time has come for the church to recognize that it has a tremendous opportunity, not only to assist older adults with such concerns as income and social services, but also to offer learning opportunities that foster hope and growth and continued meaning in their lives so that they may live more abundantly. This can be called a ministry of creative aging. The aim of this ministry is to enable people in middle and later years to build their lives in their own ways, for we were created by God to co-create.

The Concept of Creative Aging

When one thinks of creative aging, the image of a famous older artist or composer might come to mind, when, indeed, we all have the potential for creative aging. The psychotherapist Mary Baird Carlsen shares her thoughts on creativity and aging: "Here I like to think of the life of the person as a most incredible product, which will remain in production until the individual dies. The more effectively the production is maintained the more interesting and complete the product will be."[2] She further explains, "Creative aging means continuing to work with the disappointments and limitations, the 'curve balls' that life tosses our way. It means keeping our meaning as alive as possible even as our bodies lose their flexibility and stamina. It also means going beyond ourselves to see that our society and our governmental structures facilitate our freedoms within our limits. It certainly means, too, that we don't ignore the insensitivities of others, the prejudice, the unequal choices and distributions which make life more difficult for older people (and ultimately for ourselves)."[3]

This description of creative aging, then, does not focus on how artistic or how productive we are in our later years. It means discovering ourselves, in relationship with God and community, so that we may become the best "product" we can be.

Ageism—The Barrier to Creative Aging

Creative aging is not emphasized in the church, nor in society in general. This can be attributed in large part to fear and uncertainty about the aging process and about the aging experience itself. Such fear and uncertainty have resulted in the practice of ageism in society. The word *ageism*, coined by Robert Butler in 1969, seeks to express prejudice in thought and deed against older people. This negative view about aging not only affects older people themselves but younger people as well, for they may lower their goals for later life, thus interrupting the process of creative aging.

Fear and uncertainty about aging are understandable, for, after all, aging itself is a relatively new phenomenon. Never before have so many people lived to be so old. The historian Ronald Blythe suggests that a person from the Renaissance or Georgian era, able to return to our day, would be as surprised by the number of gray-haired people as by a television set. In that person's world, it was the exception to retire and to grow old. And in that time, aging was understandably associated with sickness and dependency, as this was the reality before the improvements in sanitation, public health, and medicine.[4] Today, living to a ripe and healthy old age is becoming more of an ordinary occurrence.

Gerontologists, scientists who study the process of aging, have identified some facts about our physical, psychosocial, and spiritual dimensions of health, thereby serving to dispel some of the common negative misconceptions about aging. Older people themselves are beginning to tell their stories about the uncharted territory of aging, communicating the distinct meaning and value of their later years. So, while knowledge about the aging process spreads, members of society are slowly experimenting with this novel and uncertain phenomenon of aging. It is an exciting time indeed to be aging, for it promises us the risks and opportunities of adventure and discovery.

The Wellness Model and Creative Aging

The myths of aging, which reinforce ageism in our society, are slowly being debunked through scientific evidence and through the experience of our own aging and that of others. As the walls of ageism are slowly broken down, many are coming to realize the tremendous potential for creative aging, which is possible whether we are running in marathons or confined to a wheelchair.

There is no denying that some changes with aging present a threat to one's health and well-being. However, research findings support the view that some of these changes can be modified through various interventions in the environment.

Thus, the negative illness model of aging, that one goes downhill steadily with age, is being replaced with the more positive wellness model of aging. The wellness model proposes that one can achieve wellness throughout life, despite the presence of chronic conditions and other problems which are prevalent in later life. Wellness is defined here as "a state of being, an attitude . . . more than the absence of illness . . . an ongoing process."[5] Wellness involves one's whole being, with its physical, psychological, social, and spiritual dimensions. The wellness model of aging involves the potential for change and growth in all of its dimensions, thus opening the door to creative aging. The wellness model involves taking responsibility for one's own health and keeping the faith and hope which strengthens the ability to cope with life's changes. Most important, the wellness model reflects the realities or facts about aging, rather than the myths or misconceptions. The following are some realities of the physical, psychological, social and spiritual dimensions of aging.

Physical Dimension

The misconception that to be old means to be sick can be clarified by the reality that, in spite of the inevitable physical changes of aging and associated chronic conditions, most of us can expect to continue to live in the community and to function independently. Furthermore, there is evidence that some of the physical problems of aging can be modified through the application of such health habits as diet and exercise.

Psychological Dimension

As for the intellectual changes of normal aging, the myth of senility can be put to rest. We don't become confused or "senile," which is a nonmedical term meaning mentally impaired. Most of us can expect to enjoy good mental health. In spite of psychological changes, such as increasing difficulty in recalling information from memory and taking a little longer to learn something new, we have a lifelong capacity to learn and to improve in intelligence, memory and creativity. Although there are specific strategies to do this, in general the key is participation in learning throughout life, which supports the adage "If you don't use it, you lose it." Learning also involves teaching, which encourages the sharing of experiences and ideas. It follows that as with age, we have more and more to share, we need to regard ourselves as teachers as well as learners.

Social Dimension

The myth that "most people are lonely and isolated from their families" can also be discarded. Although social relationships are diminished and it becomes more difficult to form new relationships, families still remain the primary source of relationship for older people. And when families are not available, there are numerous organizations that offer opportunities for social relationships, such as the church, which has a major role to play in this regard. Social support is especially important in our lives, for it has been shown to positively affect our health in later life. Social support in the form of informal group activity, as opposed to a more formal, structured type of activity, has been found to encourage expressions of well-being in older people. As for the social loss of work role, most people adjust well to retirement, and retirement is not harmful to one's health!

Spiritual Dimension

Finally, we come to the spiritual dimension of wellness in later life. The myth that "older people become more religious as they age" cannot be accepted, because patterns of church attendance are established early in life and remain fairly stable with age, with church membership and attendance dropping off in the 70s. So it is not correct to assume that someone is more religious because of age—it depends on the individual. Besides, being "religious" may or may not be expressed through participation in formal religious practices. For example, participation in private religious activities such as prayer, personal devotions, listening to religious music or a religious service on the radio or television is very common in older people who do not attend religious services. Religion is but one aspect of spirituality, however.

Among all the dimensions of the wellness model, the spiritual takes on the most importance as we grow older and offers the most potential for growth and change. Numerous studies show that religion and spirituality are important influences on physical, psychological, and social well-being in later life, thus lending support to the position that the spiritual dimension is the integrating part of the whole, or serves as the core of well-being. Recognizing the importance of the spiritual, scientists and theologians have intensified their efforts in the study of spirituality and aging.

A common definition of spirituality is the human longing to find meaning and purpose in life. How does this definition apply to our later years? Developmental theorists have proposed that the developmental tasks in our later years are to become whole and to reach integrity. This means that the importance of the spiritual dimension increases with age as the need to search for meaning and purpose intensifies. Erikson's concept of integrity relates to the ability to affirm the meaning and significance of one's life.[6] The psychologist Carl Jung defined the last half of life as having a purpose of its own—the development of self-awareness through reflective activity, which is a change from the concern for the survival of the species in the first half of life.[7] Butler sees reflective activity in the form of the life review as a healing activity and writes, "The old are not only taking stock of themselves as they review their lives, they are trying to think and feel through what they will do with the time that is left and with whatever emotional and material legacies they may have to give others."[8] Thus Butler views the search for meaning and significance of one's life as a potentially creative process.

Spiritual well-being was first given formal recognition as relevant to all areas of life at the 1971 White House Conference on Aging. Then, in 1972, the National Interfaith Coalition on Aging (NICA) was organized. The focus of this organization's activities is on spiritual well-being, defined as "the affirmation of life in a relationship with God, self, community and environment that nurtures and celebrates wholeness" (NICA, 1975). This definition proposes that spiritual well-being is a vital dimension to total wellness, and is a process of the validation of the gift of added years in relationship with God, self and others, thereby providing the faith and hope, which nurtures well-being. And how does one approach spiritual well-being? By helping ourselves and others discover the answers to such spiritual questions as, Why am I here? Why survive? Wellness?—for what? Creativity!—why?

The Church's Response

How, then, can the church respond to the challenge of creative aging? A major step in this direction is to offer creative educational activities that reflect the wellness model of aging, with the spiritual dimension at the core. These activities can help us to discover ourselves in relationship with God in community, so that we may become the best product we can be. These activities know no boundaries. The sky's the limit! The setting can be anywhere—church, high school, community college, nursing home, private home, or even the park! The style can be formal or informal. The group size can be small or large, but small groups of seven people are more conducive to participation, so that everyone has a chance to be heard and so that everyone can hear. The content can be no content at all. In fact, too much content and structure get in the way of self-discovery and the creative process.

The important thing to remember is to plan activities aimed at the special learning needs of the middle years and beyond. Although we become more diverse as we age, and that includes our interests, we have some learning needs in common that are based on the developmental tasks of later life. These learning needs have been categorized by Howard McCluskey as the need to cope, to express oneself, to contribute, to exert influence, and to transcend oneself.[9] These categories reflect the wellness model of aging, as they incorporate the physical, psychological, social, and spiritual dimensions of aging and, as such, can serve as a guide in the planning of educational activities in the church. A brief description of how these categories can promote creative aging, and some examples of activities, follow. The ideas for these activities come from my own experience and from those of my older friends.

Coping Needs

The physical, psychological, social, and spiritual changes of aging, coupled with an increasingly complex society, require activities that focus on coping skills. Problem-solving skills and skill-building are needed here. Learning about our aging process, for example, can help us with our coping needs. A place to begin to learn about the wellness approach to the aging process and to be an informed health consumer can be found in a book by Porterfield and St. Pierre, *Healthful Aging*. Coping with the issues of care-giving is another area of concern in our later years. Educational opportunities that can help to meet coping needs are often available at community colleges, or in other settings, and can be publicized. A discussion group integrating spiritual questions and themes can be a part of, or a follow-up to, these topics. Support groups are especially useful in helping to meet coping needs.

Expressive Needs

Expressive needs are associated with self-fulfillment through participating in activities for their own sake and not necessarily to meet a goal. Activities that focus on the humanities, such as literature, poetry, art, music, and film, can enable us to express our thoughts and feelings as we reflect on our lives, present, past, and future. Reminiscing in small groups serves to meet our expressive needs. For example, an experience with an intergenerational Lenten study using the symbols of Lent for a series of small group discussions resulted in triggering recollections of the past in several older participants The life review is also a powerful way to meet our expressive needs, which in turn nourishes the capacity to cope. This can be done through journaling, tape recording, diaries, and autobiographical writing. One resource available is a guide to discovering meaning for life through autobiographical writing, *Telling Your Story*, by B. J. Hately.[10]

Contributive Needs

It is important at any age to feel that we have something to offer to the world and that we have some influence and control. We need opportunities to achieve mastery and to enhance our self-image. We need to feel needed. We need to be invited to share our gifts in a variety of ways. And if we aren't invited to share our gifts, we need to be empowered through educational activities to break the mold and show what we can do. We need to be advocates for ourselves as well as others—and in the process, to keep a sense of humor. Here are some experiences that illustrate these points.

An older friend told me that she used to teach church school at her former church. When I asked her why she doesn't teach now, she replied, "They don't use people my age in the church school here."

My friend was not invited to teach, but then, neither did she make others aware of her gift of teaching. My friend needs encouragement by me and others to volunteer to teach in the church school.

Another friend, in her 90s at the time, was invited by the rector to teach church school as a substitute. After responding that she would do so, she overheard the rector comment to someone else, "I've really had to scrape the barrel to get a substitute for the church school." My friend's comment to me was, "Any dents in my ego have been fully compensated by the many chuckles I've had as I pictured myself sitting cross-legged in the bottom of a barrel, waiting to be scraped off!" This friend *was* invited to share her gift of teaching, and when she heard that she was asked as a last resort, she rose above it all by keeping a sense of humor.

Contributive needs can be satisfied by singing in the choir, baking for the bake sale, and serving on committees, to name a few, but let's be careful that we don't limit ourselves to only certain activities in the church community. Breaking out of our molds by exploring different ways to contribute helps us to more fully discover our talents. For example, perhaps a person who always runs the rummage sale would like to learn more about pastoral visitation. And what about older members of the church who don't seem interested in becoming involved in any activity? Perhaps a person was baptized in the church and has been attending ever since. What stories could be told! Such a person was invited to describe a display table of memorabilia from the church during a coffee hour between services. There was some lively participation around that table as people of all ages listened to the newly appointed "church historian" and shared reminiscences. Intergenerational activities are especially helpful in meeting contributive needs.

Transcendental Needs

Transcendence means rising above and beyond the limitations of physical powers and diminishing life expectancy, thus establishing a sense of meaning in one's life. Educational activities enable us to explore the existential and spiritual significance of life and living, as we ask such questions as, Why am I here? Why me? What's it all about? Who and whose am I? The use of scripture, poetry, music, and literature can move us toward transcendence by helping us to discover ourselves in relationship to God and others. In this process of nurturing the spirit, faith and hope can be strengthened. A book of meditative reflections that addresses issues of later life, such as *No Wrinkles on the Soul*, by Richard Morgan, can be useful here. Television is becoming a valuable resource for congregations to explore questions of belief and meaning. For example, the Faith and Values Channel, which represents the diversity of Judeo-Christian faith communities in the United States, offers viewers guides, as well as programs. These programs, which deal with issues of faith, ethics and values, can serve as triggers for discussion by small groups in the home or in the church. Other activities to facilitate the search for transcendence are Bible study and those mentioned earlier that aim to satisfy our expressive needs. And who can forget the power of humor to help us transcend life's problems? Laughter is a healing act and is also contagious. Humor can be incorporated into any activity, but it can also be planned. For example, a clown act might be planned for an intergenerational program, and cartoons and jokes can be included in newsletters and on bulletin boards.

Creative Aging in Action

The church is invited to offer an environment for creative aging by planning educational activities that reflect the wellness model of aging, with the spiritual dimension at the core. The program may be great or small, as illustrated by a number of examples. The Shepherd's Center model in Kansas City, Missouri, demonstrates ecumenism at work for creative aging. A parish nurse has developed a Health and Aging Ministry Program that focuses on the wellness model. A Bible study group is meeting regularly, searching for affirmation in the second half of life, thereby preparing the way for creative aging.

As for educational materials for creative aging, these are usually not labeled as such. There are many materials available, however, that deal with the issues of later life. These can be used creatively to address our common learning needs in later life as previously outlined. Churches and various secular organizations, such as the American Association of Retired Persons and the National Council on the Aging, are valuable resources for educational materials. The Episcopal Society for Ministry on Aging (ESMA) makes available *Older Adult Ministry: A Resource for Program Development*, a practical guide for program development for older adults. The Parish Nurse Resource Center is a place to start when there is an interest in health and aging ministry.

The planning of activities for creative aging, however, does not depend on the "designated education person" alone. When it comes to the selection and use of materials, who is in a better position to know what we need than ourselves? For example, one very successful group of older women formed a discussion circle at their church. They selected their book for discussion, *The Road Less Traveled*, by M. Scott Peck, after rejecting the recommendations from the pastor. They included devotions and poetry as part of the book discussion sessions. Over time, they became a support group and had so much to say that they expanded the one-hour Sunday morning session to two-and-a-half-hour sessions on Tuesdays, including the lunch hour. One person (age 94) volunteered to lead the discussions because "no one else had time," and the poetry readings and reflections were the responsibility of— guess who?—a poet! Another group of older women has developed a newsletter on aging. The newsletter includes information about issues of aging, quotes for reflection, scripture passages, poetry, and cartoons and jokes. As one explores the matter, it becomes clear that the educational approach to creative aging means involving people to participate in the educational process, not only as learners, but as planners and teachers as well. It is by participating in this way that we can move along on our own paths toward creative aging.

Notes

1.   J. Seeber, "Needed: A Ministry Trained in Aging," *Aging Connections* 9, no. 4 (1988): 238.

2.   M. B. Carlsen, M. B. *Creative Aging: A Meaning-Making Perspective* (New York: W. W. Norton, 1991), 39.

3.   Ibid., 33

4.   R. Blythe, *The View in Winter: Reflections on Old Age* (New York: Harper & Row, 1979), 3.

5.   J. Travis, *Wellness Workbook: A Guide to High Level Wellness* (Mill Valley, CA: Wellness Resource Center, 1977).

6.   E. Erikson, *Childhood and Society,* 2nd. ed. (New York: W. W. Norton, 1963).

7.   C. Jung, "The Stages of Life," in *The Portable Jung,* ed. J. Campbell, trans. R. F. C. Hall (New York: Viking Press, 1971).

8.   R. Butler, *Why Survive? Being Old in America* (New York: Harper & Row, 1975), 412.

9.   H. Y. McCluskey, "Education for Aging: The Scope of the Field and Perspectives for the Future," in *Learning for Aging,* ed. S. N. Grabowski and M. W. Dean (Washington, D. C.: Adult Education Association, 1973).

10. B. J. Hately, *Telling Your Story, Exploring Your Faith* (Order from Christian Board of Publication, Box 179, St. Louis, MO 63166).

Recommended Resources

Faith and Values Channel Program Guide. Faith and Values, 74 Trinity Place, 9th Floor, New York, NY 10006-2003.

R. Morgan, *No Wrinkles on the Soul* (Nashville: Upper Room Books, 1990).

Parish Nurse Resource Center, 1700 Western Avenue, Park Ridge, IL 60068.

J. Porterfield, and R. St. Pierre, *Healthful Aging* (Guildford, CT: Dushkin, 1992).

Shepherd's Centers of America, Suite 616, 6700 Troost Avenue, Kansas City, MO 64131.

Study Guide

Toward Creative Aging: The Church's Response

Reflection Questions

* Identify one or two people who you feel did *not* "age creatively."
  What qualities or characteristics did they have? Identify one or two
  people who, in your experience, have "aged creatively." What qualities or characteristics did they have?

* Do you hold a "wellness model" or an "illness model" of aging? How
  might your attitude toward aging influence your life-style, choices,
  health, or well-being as you get older?

* Karner lists four needs: coping, expressive, contributive and transcendental. Think about these categories, and identify your hopes
  and the fears in regard to each category as you envision your later
  years. What can/will you do to address the fears and fulfill the hopes?

* Imagine that you are 80 or 90 (or at least 10 years older than you
  now are); imagine you are in front of a mirror. What do you look
  like? The phone rings; who is it? What will you be doing today?
  What, at that age, would you want from your congregation? What
  would you like to contribute to your congregation?

* What can/will your congregation or primary Christian community do
  to help you and/or older adults address these needs?

Group Study

Step 1:   Invite the group to tell stories of ageism they have expe-
                rienced or observed. What assumptions about older
                people underlie these experiences?

Step 2:   Karner identifies myths/misconceptions in four dimen-
                sions: physical, psychological, social, and spiritual.

Invite group members to say which myths they most believe are true. Which myths do they most strongly fear?

Step 3:   Ask the group to identify the percentage of congregational members in each age group. (If you have data, make that available.) What percentage are over 60? Over 70? Over 80? Over 90? What percentage are retired? What percentage are employed? What does this information tell you about your congregation's life and ministry?

Step 4:   Karner lists four needs: coping, expressive, contributive and transcendental. Ask participants to consider: What is your congregation doing in each of these need categories? What could you do? What will you do?

Step 5:   Develop a personal and/or a group action plan for each item an individual and/or the group is committed to carry out. List all the steps that need to be taken, what each step requires (funds, materials, involvement of others), when each step will be completed, and who will be responsible for doing it. Include plans on how you will communicate progress (meetings, letters, phone calls), how you will involve others, and how you will celebrate your accomplishments.

Death Preparation as Life Enhancement

Eugene C. Bianchi

To be truthful from the start, we should admit that there is no fully adequate way to prepare for one's own death. At first blush, such an assertion would seem to deny the purpose of this essay, but in fact it may be the only honest way to begin.

Moreover, it is a sound way to launch reflection on preparing for death, because the admission of our limitations points to the power and depth of the phenomenon of death that hangs over each one of us. We would like to be able to treat death like any other important problem in life. Through science and humanistic learning, we tell ourselves, the untidy issue of dying can be worked into a schedule of priorities. But such thinking is just part of the normal self-deception that seems to help us cope with life.

We fancy ourselves to be mature adults who know about death; the media parade it before us daily, and we joke about death and taxes as the only sure things. But this is not to know real death and dying, because we are not personally involved. It is not our own death, the ultimate lonely encounter with the cessation of our own existence, with the final loss that summarizes all other losses for us personally.

Although we cannot know death in a gripping way (except for certain life-threatening events, e.g., illness, accidents, war), we can take limited, valuable steps toward preparing ourselves for it. While we are unable to deal with our death under the actual circumstances of its occurrence, we can struggle against the unhealthy modern tendency to deny death through escape and avoidance. Yet the question remains for most people: Why dwell on such a morbid subject, one that raises some of our greatest fears? The answer is quite straightforward, though still difficult to accept. It is simply that growth and deepening of personhood depends on coming to grips with mortality in a concrete, individual way.

Philosophers, theologians, and psychologists emphasize the paradox in the title of this chapter: that life can be enhanced through reflective meditation on death. In a mysterious way, what seems to be a denial of life becomes the hinge on which psychological and spiritual maturity turn. Major world religions underscore this point through a variety of symbols. For example, nearly all of Christianity's main symbols focus on the problem of death. The liturgical events of Christmas and Easter speak directly to our theme. Christmas brings hope for new life in the face of the darkness of death symbolized in the winter solstice. And Easter represents faith and hope in the victory of life over death. Such religious symbolism can be misused to hide the believer's need to struggle personally with the challenges of mortality, but Christian doctrines can also be interpreted more soundly as an invitation to enter the narrow path toward enlightenment/redemption through death.

We will divide our reflections into two sections: long-term thoughts in preparation for death and considerations when death is more proximate. Social concern underlines another important theme running through these reflections. As we accomplish the conversions or personal breakthroughs at various stages of life by encountering death, we can be freed for fuller social responsibility. We become less driven by our own survival compulsions, more aware of our common plight with the rest of creation, and freed for ethical commitments for peace and justice.

This social dimension of conversions through death-encounter is closely linked to creative aging. A great ideal of elderhood is the development of universal concerns and involvements; a mature elder has moved through neurotic fears of death to be able to embrace the major causes of humankind. These older people will be in the forefront of movements to preserve posterity and curb other dangers to physical and moral life on the planet.

Long-Term Preparation

We are so used to daily living that we miss the splendid mystery of being alive. Perhaps the greatest wonder of our experience of existence is to realize how tenuous and precarious a thing it is to be a living, feeling, thinking person. For this complex spark of life known as *homo sapiens* is surrounded by death or by the forces that lead to death. The German philosopher, Martin Heidegger has reminded us that the fundamental fact of existence is that we are creatures oriented toward death. This is not said to make us feel fearful, though that may happen when we grasp the fragility of life over against the powers of death. Nor is Heidegger simply restating a biological truism that we know from the living/dying process of all organisms. Rather, he is calling us to regain a primordial human awareness of the compelling mystery of being alive in constant contention with death.

We are only a few heartbeats or a few breaths away from the end of our existence. The philosopher wants to awaken the poet in each of us to taste the wonder of it all. When we seize upon the fact that we are contingent, not absolute or necessary beings, we start to comprehend the drama of each person's existence, suspended for a very brief moment in cosmic history between the darkness that went before and the unknown death that lies ahead. In this scenario death becomes a mystery that is both tantalizing and terrifying; it attracts our deeper curiosities and at the same time frightens us with the threat of losses that seem final. The theologian Rudolf Otto spoke of God as a mystery that both entices and terrifies. These traits are found across cultures and across historical periods. The analogy between God and death is puzzling, but it points also to an interlinking of religious sensibility and the primordial experience of being alive toward death.

When should we prepare people to appreciate this life/death mystery? Because its truth begins not in old age but at birth, childhood is the place to start. Although the earlier stages of life are not the principal focus of this essay, a few reflections are in order. It is healthy that more people today are willing to help children learn about death, in keeping with their capacities at particular ages. This means an appropriate witnessing of dying and of death, as well as a growing confidence in being able to talk about death, especially when it closely affects children, as when a friend or relative dies.

Adolescence is an especially important time to aid the young in understanding death. The teen years typically bring a turmoil of self-identity through sexual maturation and the uncertain prospects of entering an adult world. Youths in this stage are in an unusually good time to experience the mental and emotional pain of transition, of leaving behind the comforts of childhood and venturing into new terrain. Teenagers are often deeply affected by the death of a peer or by the loss of a parent.

The following period of young adulthood may be the least fertile stage for personal dialogue with death. For most people, the decades of the 20s and 30s are a time of energetic striving to establish themselves in the realms of intimacy/family and work/career. In reasonably favorable circumstances, the youthful ego does not have a keen sense of its mortality. Life seems to stretch out with unlimited horizons; signs of decline are not apparent. Sensitive young people may show a genuine interest in learning about death and dying, but this is generally not an existential concern for themselves. It may be a blessing that young adulthood is absolved from proximate concerns about death, for during this phase of life, the young must develop independence and strength of character. Their talents must blossom in vigor for the sake of civilization and of the next generation.

Of course, these are only generalizations about phases in the life span; there will be many exceptions to the typical patterns. What counts in the process of death education is adapting theory and practice to authentic insights and feelings according to phases of life. Much can be done before midlife to sensitize individuals about the challenges that will arrive in each of their lives. The seeds of psychological and spiritual growth can be planted; if young people are kept ignorant about the deeper issues, they may be unable in midlife to face the hard message of mortality. The failure of many men and women to negotiate in creative ways the physical, psychological, and social crises of middle age can be in part attributed to a lack of preparation in their younger years, for the many facets of the midlife struggle are reducible in the end to coping with one's personal mortality.

If one has not started to comprehend that this is the real reason for the malaise of the middle years, chances are that a person will accept the superficial nostrums for curing the doubts and perplexities of midlife. People will try to escape the pain of growth through hyperactivity or withdrawal from action, through new romances, through buying bigger cars or boats, or by pursuing the myriad other distractions from the real issue.

Role of Religion

Yet it is especially in midlife that the most important long-term preparation for death can happen. In the period between 40 and 60, we encounter in a very personal way our death-proneness. We start to count the years from the end rather than from the beginning. Our bodies commence to bear the signs of aging, signs that marshal before us the limits of time, energy, and, eventually, good health. Recognized or unrecognized, small "deaths" take place on various levels: Earlier dreams for a certain mode of family and intimacy may fade, or the youthful dreams of success in one's career may vanish. If we could learn to be quietly prayerful (that is, develop a habit of listening awareness) as these events assault us, we would know that we are being prepared for a new journey in the spirit.

Embracing these trials reflectively and contemplatively, we come to understand that we are going through what Gandhi called "experiments in truth." We may need a spiritual guide or a psychological counselor or a supportive group to help us weather the difficult testing. But the training that stems from death-awareness can lead us toward greater personal wholeness and outward creativity.

Religion at its best, psychology in depth, and the philosophical search for meaning are wasted on the young. Of course, this is a badly exaggerated statement. Yet it is an attempt to focus dramatically on a kernel of truth, namely, that the religious-psychological-philosophical seeker can embrace the hard experience of paradox, mystery, and depth only when he or she is ready for it. Given our lust for life and our unconscious fear of death, it is unlikely that we will be ready for the new journey before middle age, when, like it or not, the footsteps of O'Neill's iceman sound more distinct to us.

Admittedly, there is a certain fear, perhaps even terror, involved in allowing intimations of our own death into our minds and hearts. The contrast in midlife is particularly shocking; we may be at the apex of energies and accomplishments, while the signs of old age and death declare themselves in graying hair and wrinkles. These experiences can be great turning points in life. Will we make the transitions of mind and soul away from the narrower dreams of youth and toward lives of fuller introspection, empathy, and compassionate commitment to wider concerns of humanity?

Introspection, contemplation, and inwardness are relatively foreign notions in our culture. Yet they are indispensable in finding one's truer self in midlife. There can be no death preparation as life enhancement without some cultivation of an inward life. This does not mean giving up active pursuits in one's career and social life. Rather, it involves dedicating some time, preferably each day, to helpful forms of solitary contemplation.

Many simple techniques for quieting and centering are available in books, as well as in course offerings and private instruction. Even as little as 10 or 15 minutes a day of silence and solitude can fulfill this purpose; but one must be motivated to make that time as sacred and intentional as the most important of life's activities. This gradual, personal journey beyond our fearfully controlling ego-consciousness allows us to break through the facades that hide us from ourselves, that is, from the deeper reaches of our souls.

Some of these periods of prayerful listening to inner voices may be dry, tedious, and distressing. This may be especially true in midlife, when thoughts of losses, failures, paths not taken, and the curtailing of time press in on us. These kinds of seemingly negative experiences, joined to the occasional dryness or apparent sterility of contemplative periods, are the narrow passages that may lead us to the edge of doubt and ambivalence about life. Yet these dark nights of the soul, as the mystics referred to them, are the points of encounter with death in life. In Jungian language, this can be represented as the ego learning hard but necessary lessons from its deeper self; in classical lore it is portrayed in the figure of Hermes, the youthful, active messenger, sitting at the feet of Hades to learn the secrets of the underworld.

The encounter with one's finitude in the middle years, whether expressed in psychological or religious idiom, is an event at once illuminating and painful. One becomes more familiar with the neglected opposites within one's own personality: shadow aspects, repressed child, devouring mother, rejected feminine or masculine sides.

From a religious standpoint, the suffering facets of these encounters can be ways of symbolically meeting the crucified deity within, the God who is a suffering fellow traveler in our inmost soul. In all of this, we are dealing directly with death as woven into the very fabric of existence. Sometimes these moments of solitude and contemplation will be filled by a void of calming peace; at such moments the broken strands of our life, our old wounds, find a healing balm.

Meditation on death puts us in touch with our finitude; in the middle years an experience of finitude can be the catalyst for developing one's own religiousness or spirituality. This is not a flight in desperation to a religious solution out of personal fears. Rather, an encounter with our own finitude, by making us more conscious of intellectual, physical, and moral limitations, tends to make relative the hold of institutions over us. The "oughts" of church, family, occupation, and the state are less constraining. We understand, perhaps for the first time, that in the end we must take responsibility for our own decisions and actions.

Developing one's own spirituality needs the insights of tradition and a renewed grasp of the values mirrored in history. But these insights and values are appropriated in ways congruent with personal conscience; they are not merely rules imposed from without. Although it might seem that cultivating one's own spirituality is an eminently individual process, the surprising truth is that important social consequences flow from the contemplation of finitude.

By freeing us from a rigid, external code of conduct, such contemplation enables us to criticize institutions and regulations as we work toward humanizing them and adapting them to current needs. Moreover, by being less bound to conventions of thought and action, we are opened to new levels of creativity. Instead of using energy to defend ourselves against threatening ideas or challenging persons, we can allow novel events to enter into conversation with a self-directed personality that knows the limits of all things.

At the heart of this development of one's own spirituality through reflection on one's finitude is a deeper experience of faith. Faith is frequently misunderstood as a collection of beliefs connected with certain moral practices and rituals. Yet faith must be distinguished from these religious manifestations. Faith is an attitude and act of profound trust in the face of death with its ultimate threat of annihilating all meaning. Faith is an action of releasing the walled-off self into communion with a benevolent and sustaining Reality that pervades a death-oriented cosmos. In its depths, it is a kind of letting-go that only that person can perform who understands from his or her own life the final transitoriness of all things.

At this level, beliefs and practices assume a new position in our outlook; they may be carriers of meaning and grace inasmuch as they are suffused by faith. The faith that flows from meditation on death also liberates the imagination to craft and embrace a fuller unity in pluralism that transcends the narrow barriers of nation, race, and creed.

Finally, such faith keeps us from falling into the paralysis and disintegration that afflict many who are not able to cope with the indications of their own aging and death. A kind of psychological death occurs when an individual tries to deny the signs of finitude in neurotic modes of withdrawal from life or of heedless plunging into youthful activities. Such a person is clinging fearfully to life as a possession to be defended against death, rather than as a gift to be shared to the end. Faith gives one the courage to break through those temptations and infuse life with hope and meaning in ever-richer ways as death approaches.

Social Aspects of Reflections on Death

Long-term education in light of death might seem to be a very private affair. This essay has stressed the personal dimension of this introspection, but the social aspects of such reflection have great significance. Among modern thinkers, Ernest Becker makes one of the strongest cases for the link between fear of death and social evils. He depicts a powerful, unconscious motivation to repress the terrors of death by defending ourselves and our immediate group at any cost to others. Humans all too eagerly transfer their independence and self-initiative to leaders who promise to protect them against dangers to life. This concentration of power in hierarchies causes leaders to abuse outsiders who threaten the tribe and to oppress their own people.

At the root of Becker's explanation of personal and social evil is the all-pervasive fear of one's own death, coupled with a relentless desire for immortality. Fearful anxiety before the world's overwhelming perils calls for the spilling of blood and other hurtful actions to expiate guilt and gain immortal life. Cruelty to outsiders becomes a kind of torture rite that convinces the perpetrators of their own life power, while denying it to others. We do in our fellow humans out of the fear of losing our own lives.

Although Becker's views merit critical comment and much nuancing, they dramatize an all-too-pervasive tendency in individuals and groups to preserve ourselves at terrible costs to others. Yet we need to know the worst in us to realize possibilities for the best. Along the introspective journey of meeting the terror of death, we can be transformed into persons who see and act in ways directly opposed to destructiveness. Through this kind of gradual education, death can become an ambiguous guest in our souls, inspiring both fear and hope. While we will always be anxious about our own death, we can come to understand the common bonds of our creaturehood, our fellowship with death-prone humanity and nature.

When this experience is graced by the faith described earlier, potentials for empathy and compassion arise. We experience ourselves as companions with others in survival, rather than competitors for a chimerical immortality. Thus an ethical orientation arising out of a continuing dialogue with death as both fearful and wisdom-bearing could lead to a new spirit of empathy, of sharing and of cohumanity.

This new ethical spirit, born out of personal conversion through encounter with finitude, manifests itself in midlife as we begin to see our professional and other commitments in a new light. Work becomes more than simply a means for escaping deeper questioning or for immortalizing ourselves through dominance over persons and nature. Rather, our work evolves toward being a flexible means for spiritual exploration and for service of a wider community.

The ideal is that of a contemplative in action, a person fully involved in the world, yet not seeking to possess it for purely personal ends. This implies a spiritual transformation of work that allows us to appreciate and enjoy worldly matters for their own sake, while we seek to surround them with the structures of truth and justice. Our life becomes ever more outwardly focused in service and in being mentors to others, while at the same time our inner life is enriched.

This is not some airy and unattainable ideal. Dag Hammarskjöld, an early secretary general of the United Nations, left a rich spiritual journal, *Markings*, that depicts his inward transformations while his days were outwardly consumed in serving as an international statesman. Hammarskjöld, who died in a plane crash while negotiating a dispute in Africa, also witnesses in his journal to a growing understanding of the meaning of his life in terms of his own finitude.

Dorothy Day, pacifist and servant of the urban dispossessed, through her writings and her activities in the Catholic Worker Movement, also left a testament of profound contemplation in action. Her memoirs, *The Long Loneliness*, reveal the transitions of a soul increasingly dedicated to charitable actions and at the same time deepening her own inner life in a spirit of radical contingency.

Intrinsic to developing the social compassion and commitment previously noted is a change of attitude toward power. The exercise of mental, emotional, and physical power or energy is part of what it means to be human. Youth stresses the exercise of power as mastery or dominance to protect and enhance the ego. Problems arise when this mode of power becomes the sole way of relating to the world for the whole life span. Technological society accentuates dominant power through the manipulation and control of external reality.

Fear of death, the greatest loss of power, all too frequently leads to injustices and other forms of destructiveness. The social evils deriving from hatred, malice, and selfishness are connected with our understanding of power as dominance.

The shift from dominant power to serving or enabling power is closely linked to a creative dialogue with death and finitude in midlife. In this dialogue we realize how futile and destructive has been our embracing of dominant power to preserve ourselves against various forms of death. As we find the faith to let go of self-preservation, we also discover forgiveness for our immersion in the violence of dominant power over others. We move gradually to cultivate a kind of eliciting or enabling power that allows others to respond authentically and humanely.

This nonviolent power represents a significant change in our attitude toward the world. We no longer seek to use self-serving force, but in the charity that seeks union with what is loved, we allow others genuinely to exercise their own energies. Perhaps this is one of the greatest experiences to which persons in midlife are invited: to substitute, for the power that promises to preserve the ego against adversity and death, a new power that, by releasing us from the all-consuming lust for self-survival, allows us joyful love of our deepest self and of others.

Meditation on personal death can also become an occasion for deepening our friendships and intimacies. When we become conscious of unhealthy defenses against death, in faith we can release some of our fearfulness. As we do this, our attitude toward family and friends can change; we can permit more of our true selves, with our illusions and vulnerabilities, to appear.

When we realize that time is not on our side, we can risk mutual revelation, trusting that the other can support the truth about ourselves. We long to reach beyond appearances, to touch and be touched by others at the center of our being. Knowing our common mortality can expand our sense of compassion and care. The middle-aged, for example, can reach out across generations to respect and stimulate the potential of younger people and to relate with care to the older generation. In this process of enriching our friendships as we encounter our own finitude, there is a paradoxical joining of pain and joyfulness. It is painful to become more accepting of our weaknesses, hostilities, and self-deceptions; yet, when we have been educated in the school of death, we can also regard more lightly matters that we might otherwise take too seriously.

In a seemingly contradictory way, an ability to invest one's work with a certain zest, lightness, and humor depends on a personal acceptance of death. We know in a new way that our activities will not ultimately preserve us; work, then, divested of false expectations can become a form of play, especially if it is conducive to one's personal growth.

What we have said about middle age concerning preparation for death as life-enhancing can continue to be the basis for a creative elderhood. But the last phase of life, from about 60 onward, has its own particular qualities. Death itself becomes a more proximate reality than it was previously. New limits and diminishments may gradually depress persons, especially if they have known good health throughout life. Losses of friends and intimates further impact on elders. Many suffer a loss of role significance through retirement; others with limited economic means worry about basic health care and adequate living conditions for themselves and their families.

Moreover, these new problems of older age must be faced in an ageist society, which advances negative stereotypes about being old. The elderly may themselves embrace these debasing attitudes, thus bringing about a premature sort of psychic dying that opposes dealing with death constructively. Any combination of these considerable challenges can pull an elderly person downward into depression, hopelessness, self-deceit, flight into the past, loneliness, and a general withdrawal from vital living.

Growth Through Diminishment

These are some of the real dangers of elderhood, and they are exemplified all too often in the contemporary world. Precisely because these issues have such dire consequences in old age, the personal transitions of attitude and spirit from midlife on take on paramount importance.

If transformation of values progresses from middle age, there is a good chance for what Teilhard de Chardin called "growth through diminishments." Refined in the crucible of their own sufferings and sacrifices, such elders are gradually purified of egotism but develop fuller self-esteem. Their trials teach them greater truthfulness that lessens self-deception and makes them wise guides for others. They seem able to infuse their lives with quality time, even when the quantity of sand is smaller in the top of the hourglass. Instead of the inflexibility sometimes associated with the old, these elders go through a self-reidentification process. This means fulfilling some of the needs and desires that went unrealized in earlier years. To summarize these gracious developments in such older people, we can say that in the very face of death they experience a greater freedom from the fear of death.

What needs to be stressed, however, for these spiritually advanced elderly persons is their calling toward universal concerns. The tendency of our culture is to confine the elderly to private pursuits at the periphery of societal life. As the older person is pushed out of the centers of action and decision making, outstanding skills, talents, and insights are lost to the community. The vocation of older people is to go beyond advocating merely the interests of their elderly peers to take on a spirit of stewardship for all life. With less to lose and fewer egotistical compulsions, these humanely advanced older people can achieve the apex of their careers as reconcilers. Reconciliation of destructive alienation at all levels of existence is perhaps the greatest New Testament ideal, seen in the Sermon on the Mount and in the letters of Paul (Gal. 3 and Eph. 2).

This reconciling work can take many forms, such as educational efforts toward needy young people or special services toward the elderly, especially those who are frail, confined, and poor. The elderly must also take up positions of leadership and consultation in secular and religious organizations. This does not mean that it is wrong for the old to enjoy privacy, leisure, and other pleasures. Rather, it is a matter of emphasis and responsibility.

The elderly have a wonderful contribution to make to the great needs of the world through their knowledge and expertise in many fields. Moreover, the elderly have a special calling to work as reconcilers concerning the great issues facing humanity: questions of war and peace, justice and human rights, nuclear dangers, and population/ecological matters. This task of reconciliation and peacemaking can also be accomplished in quiet, personal ways through direct contacts with other individuals and through the courage and kindness that many older people show in sickness and hardship.

In these ways, the downward physical slope of life can become an upward spiritual ascent for self and others. Such peacemaking elders have a real future for themselves in the quality of their last phase, in their contributions to those who will succeed them; and for the faithful, many also find a future in hope for a life with God after earthly death. Most elders will need support systems—formal and informal, age-integrated and age-homogeneous—to help them realize these noble goals.

When we speak of the old embracing universal concerns and returning to the centers of decision making, we are referring mainly to those increasing populations who enjoy reasonably good health into their later years. Yet there are also many with physical limitations who continue in elderhood the works of reconciliation; these are the persons who have successfully negotiated the psychospiritual transitions of midlife and the period sometimes called that of the "young old."

This creative aging differs in important ways from visions of longevity propagated in current literature on life-extension. The latter stresses quantitative dimensions of living longer; yet what finally matters is the quality of life in the last season. It is ultimately a matter of beauty, of building a mosaic with one's life. In Heidegger's idiom, this means learning gradually to dwell poetically in the world. Since great poets have always been able to express the human dilemma with finer clarity than the rest of us, we can sum up these perspectives in the words of William B. Yeats:

> An aged man is but a paltry thing,
> A tattered coat upon a stick, unless
> Soul clap its hands and sing, and louder sing
> For every tatter in its mortal dress.
> *Sailing to Byzantium*

Proximate Preparation for Death

When the scriptures tell us that we know not the day nor the hour, they remind us about a sober truth concerning death. Though we are certain that we will die, the actual event will always remain something of a surprise. This is an important note to keep before us as we address proximate preparation for death.

For most of us there will probably be a gradual passage from long-term to proximate encounter with our own dying. We may sense a substantial weakening of organic functions; chronic illnesses may hold stronger sway; we will probably have intimations that the end is not far off. This dying trajectory will be shorter for some when accidents, strokes, or heart attacks intervene. In addition to pain, fatigue, and other hardships, the approach of death will make us more dependent on others. In a culture that prizes independence and self-determination, new dependency will induce feelings of being a burden, of being valueless. The dying process, therefore, will deeply test one's sense of self-worth and self-respect.

An important preparation for these final phases of life consists in putting one's house in order in very practical affairs. This may mean writing or updating a will. It can also involve such concrete aspects as making sure that survivors know where to find documents, keys, and accounts. How do we want to dispose of our bodies: through burial, cremation, or donation to medical or scientific study? Many shy away from dealing with such issues, sometimes out of negligence, but probably as often out of fear of facing their own deaths. Yet these pragmatic matters are significant occasions for gaining perspective on optimal ways to use remaining time; moreover, these mundane concerns provide the context for showing love and care for others.

Focusing on such questions may also have the salutary effect of reminding us to finish personal business, that is, bring to closure uncompleted relationships inasmuch as we can. We may need to receive or grant forgiveness, to heal wounds still festering in our souls, or to tell others that we love and appreciate them. Various forms of life-review have been developed to aid individuals with a counselor or in groups to search personal history for points of trauma, transition, and overall meaning.

In our age of heightened medical technology, we must think ahead about extraordinary measures to sustain our existence. The controversies concerning living wills and methods of euthanasia have raised ethical questions in many circles. But ultimately we must decide for ourselves, while we are still in a position to reflect consciously on the question.

Living wills are not legally enforceable in all states, but a clear statement to kin or doctors may well influence how life-preserving technology is used. Husbands and wives, elderly parents and their children, and all others who will exercise special responsibility in such decision making should explore moral and humanistic aspects of dying with dignity. The quality of life becomes a crucial factor in determining whether it should continue.

While direct euthanasia is fraught with potential for abuse, the pain and disability of individuals (some long before the imminent coming of physical death) may so lessen the meaning of life for them that a merciful death is preferable. Dialogue on these issues may curtail guilt, remorse, and depression for those survivors who were involved in the decision to terminate life-sustaining mechanisms.

It is difficult to know beforehand how we will react when we learn that our situation is terminal. "Terminal" may mean months or perhaps a longer period; it may be signaled by a newly discovered disease or by a gradual breakdown through chronic ailments. Of course, we understand that we are all in a terminal state, but when death becomes proximate and relatively certain, intense psychological reactions often occur. It may be helpful, therefore, in preparing to meet death in a way that fosters gracious final living, to rehearse some typical responses to the announcement that death is imminent.

Moreover, the emotional reactions and defense mechanisms need to be personalized as much as possible: How do *I* generally respond to bad news, to traumatic events? A common early reaction is fear and depression or sadness; that which is most precious to us, life, is about to be lost. We fear the deterioration, pain, and incapacity that may accompany the last part of our journey. We commence grieving over the loss of family, friends, and future.

Imaginative meditation can partially summon up these feelings. In quiet contemplation on our own last trajectory, we can acknowledge painful emotions, giving them a rightful place without denial or distraction. By permitting these feelings to come alive concretely (in reference to particular persons, our own body, etc.) in meditation, we can eventually arrive at an attitude of letting go.

This letting go is a form of acceptance that brings a measure of inner peace. It is not a passive resignation to the destructive course of an illness. Rather, by working through some of these difficult emotions, we may be better able to marshal healing energies to resist the disease. A kind of emptying out of excessive fears is a necessary precondition for the type of meditative healing methods fostered by the Simontons in the book *Getting Well Again*.[1]

Still other emotions challenge one whose death is proximate. Anger, whether expressed covertly or openly, will frequently arise. A primitive but useful function of anger is the mobilization of physical and mental energies to defend against attack. Whether we rage against God, humans, or natural forces, the true meaning of this anger is a gathering of energy to cope with the deadly reality, to maintain a sense of self-meaning and integrity to the end.

The anger may be more intense if the afflicted person is younger; a sense of injustice may prevail about a life cut off before its full flowering. Anger may fluctuate with depression and feelings of guilt; we may be guilty about being angry at relatives and attendants.

Some experience guilt for seeming to cause their own illness, or because they see the condition as a punishment from God. They may also feel guilty for having to abandon their responsibilities toward family and friends. Feelings of shame further aggravate the emotional response to one's own dying. We may be ashamed of our physical condition; we know that others do not like to associate with persons who look bad, who may be incontinent, tired, and depressed. Shame can stalk the dying who worry about their unusual behavior and their increasing dependence.

Can we in meditative imagination pass before ourselves anger, guilt, and shame, as these reactions would be demonstrated in our own way? Can we think of concrete instances in which we have experienced these feelings and then transpose these reactions in imagination to our dying process? Such contemplative working-through over a period of time may prevent an excessive acting out of these emotions in the actual situation of dying.

Dealing with one's own death as a proximate happening is one of the most powerful challenges we will ever face. In light of this threat to the psyche, we must learn to respect the coping mechanisms in ourselves and others, as we try to adjust to the imminent reality of death. Various forms of denial, for example, have a positive purpose in that they allow an individual to rally energies for the confrontation.

Denial, whether direct or indirect, can be an appeal for time to muster one's forces for grappling with the final mystery of life. Some may even carry on a pretense of denial to the very threshold of death, although they know interiorly that they are moribund. This is not an ideal way to die, but it may be a mode of courage for those who do not want to upset loved ones. On the other hand, there are clearly negative dimensions to denial. It can keep a person from completing unfinished business on material and human levels; it may very well hinder the individual's ability to heighten the quality of life before death.

One's way of communicating with terminally ill people should be such as to permit the dying person to initiate discussion of the situation. Being present to the dying in a natural and caring style may elicit the deeper conversation, while respecting the boundaries of that person's integrity.

We dwell on these psychological reactions in the dying process to deepen our empathy. It is not enough to know the clinical patterns concerning death nor to amass data about the best places for the dying time. While there are important differences regarding home, hospital, or hospice care for terminally ill people, the overriding issue for our benefit and that of the dying is to learn empathy for the life phase that most of us will experience.

Such understanding is very difficult to attain, because we find it hard to reflect with realism and sympathy on this frightening phase of existence. Yet if we learn empathy through meditation on death and through visiting or working with frail or terminal persons, we will be better able to sustain their dignity in the last season. As our fear of the dying process diminishes, we become sources of security and even hope for the dying. Helping others to die with dignity and hope can be enhanced by a spirit of faith.

The latter may take the more traditional forms of religious language, or it may be expressed in less familiar idiom. The last hours of Aldous Huxley's life, for example, are movingly described in his wife's memoirs, *This Timeless Moment*. Laura Huxley performs a kind of verbal liturgy at her husband's deathbed. She encourages him, as he had done for others, to let himself go, to release himself toward the light.

The Huxley reference is just one example of the many rituals of death that can have rich meaning for terminal persons while they are still alive as well as for their survivors. Surely we can all cite certain funeral rites that have been inappropriate, superficial, or hypocritical. But the need persists to surround the great moments of life with a special time and place, with dramatic memorials that make sacred these major passages. These communal celebrations, when done with sensitivity and respect, aid the survivors to accept losses, to be upheld in grief and mourning, and eventually to be welcomed back into full engagement in life. We are beings who create meaning through symbol and story.

Although the dying time is often filled with weakness, distress, and possibly pain, it can also become the hour of final reenactment in which we strive to gather into a healing wholeness the disparate strands of life. These rituals, whether formal or informal, can be touchstones of our finest humanity. A dying young nurse was calling for the simplest of these rituals when she said to the hospital attendants:

> I know, you feel insecure, don't know what to say, don't know what to do. But please believe me, if you care, you can't go wrong. . . . Don't run away. . . . All I want to know is that there will be

someone to hold my hand when I need it. I am afraid. Death may
be routine to you, but it is new to me. . . . If only we could be
honest, both admit of our fears, touch one another. If you really
care, would you lose so much of your valuable professionalism if
you even cried with me? Just person to person? Then, it might
not be so hard to die.

Conclusion

Reflection on death, especially on one's own death, in long-term or
in proximate scenarios, can enrich the aging process. Contemplation
of personal death can spur one on to make the most of the present,
whatever one's age. Such contemplation is not an exercise in morbid-
ity for those who have started to work through the transitional crises of
midlife. My death, while always fear-inspiring in some ways, can also
be seen as part of the natural cycle of all living creatures. Christians
can learn a corrective lesson from naturalists on this point.

Christianity has so emphasized the tragic dimension of death as a
consequence of sin that it often loses sight of the natural aspect of
dying as part of planetary rhythm and obscures an equally valid biblical
perspective. For the doctrine of creation focuses on the goodness of
the natural order, including its cycles of birth and death. Although the
evil results that flow from sinful proclivities can bring about tragic and
premature physical death (e.g., crimes, wars, ecological destruction),
the main connection between sin and death is on the level of the
human spirit.

The truly dire consequence of sinfulness is death of the spirit, the
dehumanizing of individuals and groups, not the death of the body as a
natural event. Our physical life today results from billions of years of
cosmic evolution, marked by constant patterns of birthing and perish-
ing, of spring and winter. The linking of death with sin is a very recent
phenomenon, in evolutionary terms; the death that has any meaning in
this context is the demise of human potential to know and love in the
most human way.

A comprehensive view of death for persons of faith places it within
the natural, God-established order of the universe. Acceptance of this
mode of coming to be and of passing on becomes an act of fidelity to

God's providence. Such reflection helps us develop a mystic sense of belonging to a greater whole, of being part of a trustworthy purpose in the world as we make our particular contribution to what English philosopher, Alfred North Whitehead called the "creative advance."

On one level, this style of meditating on death puts us in touch with Lovejoy's vision of the chain of being: Our living and dying is joined with the life and death of all other creatures in that we mutually influence one another. In this view, our deaths serve to fertilize the garden of earth.

On another plane, we can enter early into our dying by way of personal trust. This approach is expressed graphically in a memorable story told by Lawrence Jones about an experience with his son: The mode of trust in God concerning our death is represented through an analogical experience of child-parent trust:

Down at Fisk University we had a stone wall that ran the length of the campus. My son used to like to get up on that and run. Sometimes he would run along in the evening near huge oak trees that hung over Eighteenth Avenue. There was a light in between, so that there was light and shadow. He would get up on the fence and run along in the light. Then when he got to the darkness he would jump down and take my hand. We would walk through the darkness together until we got to the light again. Then he would jump on the wall again and run. That began for me to be analogy to our relationship with God. My son knew the father that he saw in the light and whose hand he held in the dark would not change because the circumstances had changed.[2]

Whether described in traditional religious idiom or in other ways, a personal, meditative encounter with our own dying can enhance life as a time of adventure and celebration. When our living is enfolded within the mantle of the acceptance of death, each day has the potential for being a new venture. Every night we can prayerfully seek to free our minds from crushing or paralyzing events of the past, so that each morning begins a day of novel opportunities, of new beginnings. This is not a Pollyanna escape from our history; the latter should always be present to us with its lessons for life. The point is rather that as we open ourselves to a listening dialogue with death, the wounds and failures of the past impede us less from venturing hopefully into each new day.

In this sense, even our dying day can be approached as a new happening, an adventure. If life has been a series of adventures for a person, death may be looked upon as a door to still other revealing experiences. This attitude arises from a spirit of faith and hope in the benevolent energy and presence of God. Such a spirit is not necessarily a flight from facing death in the hard reality of its suffering and diminishments; nor is it a childish demand that God reward us with life everlasting because we have been good on earth. Rather, it is a serene conviction that the best of us passes on into a new adventure within the One who is greater and more beautiful than we, to paraphrase a statement of Teilhard de Chardin.

It may seem strange to speak of death as a final celebration of life. Yet that is precisely the paradox of faith. Perhaps the greatest grace we will ever experience is that of celebrating what has been and what is, as we draw near to our death. This is a special gracing for which our whole life can be a preparation. To celebrate is to rejoice for having experienced life with its pains and joys, to be glad that we have helped our survivors to preserve and nourish the beautiful, fragile gift of life into yet another season. In his spiritual memoirs Dag Hammarskjöld summed up perfectly this embracing of the world in celebration at death: "Night is drawing nigh; for all that has been, thanks; for all that shall be, yes."[3]

Notes

1.   Carl Simonton et al., *Getting Well Again* (New York, Bantam, 1982).

2.   Eugene Bianchi, *Aging as a Spiritual Journey* (New York: Crossroad, 1982), 250.

3.   Dag Hammarskjöld, *Markings* (New York: Alfred A. Knopf, 1964), 89.

Study Guide
Death Preparation as Life Enhancement

Reflection Questions

* Imagine yourself dying in the way you would least like to experience. What is happening? Who is present? What is your worst fear? What makes you feel shame? Guilt? Anger?

* Now imagine yourself dying in the way you would most like to experience. What is happening? Who is present? What are your feelings?

* Many people hope to die quickly and quietly while asleep so they do not have to face their own death. If this is what you hoped for in response to the second question, take time to imagine how you would like to die if you knew you were dying. How would you spend your last days? Whom would you want to see during that time? Who would you want to be with you when you died? What would you want them to do during your last hour?

* Bianchi says that it is important to reflect on our death because it draws us from our everyday tasks into an appreciation for the mystery of life and the mystery of death. How do you experience that mystery? How have you experienced and/or understood the paradox "that life can be enhanced through reflective meditation on death?"

* Becker "depicts a powerful, unconscious motivation to repress the terrors of death by defending ourselves and our immediate group at any cost to others." Do you see any link between the violence in our society and the repression of the terrors of death? In what ways might different people be "violent," consciously or unconsciously? Do you see that dynamic in people you know? In yourself?

* Bianchi says that the elderly have a special calling to work as reconcilers—both in the great issues facing humanity and in personal issues. Where do you feel brokenness—in the world, in your own life? How might you be a reconciler in those situations? How might your congregation, friends, family be partners with you in that work?

Group Process

Step 1:   Hubert Humphrey spoke to the Senate shortly before his death, to say that he had a need to set the record straight. He spoke about his role in supporting the Vietnam War and how he decided to support the president. He later believed he had been wrong.

Setting the record straight, and leaving a "last will and testament"—not about our material possessions, but about our most deeply held values and beliefs, the guiding principles we have forged from a lifetime of living, is something important to all of us, whether we live it out or not.

Ask each participant to write his or her own "Ethical Will and Testament." (This might be considered, as it was called at a certain university, "the last great lecture series.") Introduce this activity by saying, "If you could give your last great lecture, what would you say?"

Note: Orthodox Judaism has a heritage of the "Ethical Will," which was written for the family and printed on beautiful paper. We might well pick up this custom and pass it on, along with our wisdom.

Step 2:   Ask group members to select two people to share whatever they choose from what they have written. Ask each triad to identify items they would like to suggest for a group list.

Step 3:   Ask the group to prepare a group "ethical will and testament" listing on newsprint those values, beliefs, guiding principles and perspectives to which all group members can subscribe as an important heritage to pass on to your congregation.

Step 4:   Ask one member of the group to submit this list for inclusion in a publication of your congregation. Ask for feedback from members of the church. (*Note:* This could lead to another session for people who are not part of the present group.)

Further Reading

Henry C. Simmons

This bibliography gives a sampling of writings in the field of religion and aging, including some more recent writings. It is not a comprehensive bibliography in two regards. First, virtually all the references are from the religious sector; thus, general writings on aging, care-giving, leisure, the aging of parents, and so on, are not included. Second, the list reflects, inevitably, the interests, hunches, and perspectives of the compiler. For a fully comprehensive bibliography of aging and religious/denominational materials, the reader is directed to the book by H. Simmons and V. Pierce listed below. With its update, it is a comprehensive guide to books, articles, and dissertations from 1876 to the present.

Aging and the Human Spirit Newsletter. Institute for Medical Humanities, the University of Texas Medical Branch, Galveston, TX, 77555-1311. Edited by T. R. Cole and H. R. Moody, this newsletter addresses issues of significance for those whose care is the human spirit.

Becker, A. H. 1986. *Ministry with Older Persons: A Guide for Clergy and Congregations.* Minneapolis: Augsburg. Contains basic information on the aging process as well as practical guidelines for developing an effective ministry with older persons.

Bianchi, E. 1984. *Aging as a Spiritual Journey.* New York: Crossroad. Written primarily from a Jungian perspective, this book begins the journey of aging at midlife. Its themes are rich and complex.

Birren, J. and D. Deutchman. 1991. *Guiding Autobiography Groups for Older Adults: Exploring the Fabric of Life.* Baltimore, MD: Johns Hopkins University Press, 146 pp. The carefully researched and tested method presented in this book for strengthening the fabric of life of older adults is set forth step-by-step. The goal of the process is that the older adult sees life as meaningful and something to be proud of.

Boucher, T. 1991. *Spiritual Grandparenting: Bringing Our Grandchildren to God.* New York: Crossroads, 144 pp. Topics include deepening the meaning of holidays and visits, story and history-sharing skills, life-giving activities, love in situations of crisis, and respectful love for the parents of grandchildren.

Chinen, A.B. 1989. *In the Ever After: Fairy Tales and the Second Half of Life.* Wilmette, IL: Chiron. From 15 fairy tales in which the protagonists are older adults, the author draws out a psychology and spirituality of maturity, revealing the developmental tasks of the second half of life. His psychoanalytic and Jungian perspectives yield a rich interpretation of old age.

Cole, T. R., and S.A. Gadow, eds. 1986. *What Does It Mean to Grow Old? Reflections from the Humanities.* Durham, NC: Duke University Press. Prominent scholars from various disciplines of the humanities (philosophy, history, theology, sociology, law) reflect on the meaning of aging and death. The perspective from which they begin allows them to grasp some profoundly human aspects of aging that have an openness to the dimension of life often referred to as religious. This collection of essays is of great importance.

Cole, T. R., W. A. Achenbaum, P. L. Jakobi and R. Kastenbaum, eds. 1993. *Voices and Visions of Aging: Toward a Critical Gerontology.* New York: Springer. "Critical theory is concerned with identifying possibilities for emancipatory social change, including positive ideals for the last stage of life" (p. xv). Such inquiry undergirds a grounded spirituality.

Coupland, S. 1985. *Beginning to Pray in Old Age.* Cambridge, MA: Cowley. Well grounded in Christian tradition, this book addresses the special concern of parishioners who seek to begin or renew their lives of prayer later in life.

Facility Directory. 1994. Available from the Episcopal Society for Ministry on Aging, this resource lists the various types of Episcopal church-related housing in the United States and includes information on patients' rights and a checklist for use in selecting an appropriate facility.

Fisher, K. 1985. *Winter Grace.* New York: Paulist. Chapters deal with dependence and independence, love and sexuality, humor and hope, loss, dying, and resurrection—and the transformation of life by the gospel.

Folliet, J. 1983. *The Evening Sun: Growing Old Beautifully.* Trans. D. Smith, Chicago: Franciscan Herald. Translated from French, this charming series of 40 brief meditations is so specific to the life and culture of its author that the reader gets a glimpse of the way age, spirituality, and culture are intertwined. It serves as a model for journal writing that reflects finely honed, mature wisdom.

Glass, J. C., ed. 1988. *Educational Gerontology: Special Issue on Religion and Aging* 14 (4). "This issue looks at a number of topics about the role religion and religious education have played, are playing, and can play in responding to the concerns and needs of older adults" (p. iii).

Gray, R. H. 1984. *Survival of the Spirit: My Detour Through a Retirement Home.* Atlanta, GA: John Knox. Using excerpts from her diary, a woman who fought to maintain her individuality and personhood in a retirement home presents her struggles with grace, with compassion, and with strength.

Hargrave, T., and W. Anderson. 1992. *Finishing Well: Aging and Reparation in the Intergenerational Family.* New York: Brunner/Mazel, 208 pp. Part 1 of this book deals with the therapeutic challenge of understanding families with aging members, with such intergenerational issues as death, emotional loss, and grandparenthood. Part 2 deals with the beginning stages of the therapeutic process—life validation, life review, and therapeutic intervention.

Helfgott, K. 1992. *Older Adults Caring for Children: Intergenerational Child Care.* Washington, DC: Generations United, 119 pp. This detailed and carefully researched "how to" book shows how to plan and implement a successful intergenerational child care program, including sections on older adults caring for children, recruiting, training, and placing older adults in child care settings.

Hiltner, S., ed. 1975. *Toward a Theology of Aging.* New York: Human Sciences Press. This special issue of *Pastoral Psychology* (Winter 1974) studies psychological, sociohistorical, and theological meaning of aging in human life. Virtually all of these essays would warrant publication today on their own merits.

Howse, W. L., comp. 1990. *Senior Adult Learner's Notebook.* Nashville: Convention Press, 176 pp. In six chapters, with 38 charts and forms, this comprehensive resource book shows how to build a senior adult ministry.

Jacobs, R. H. 1987. *Older Women: Surviving and Thriving.* (Available from Family Services America, 11700 West Lake Park Drive, Milwaukee, WI 53224.) Twelve workshop sessions designed to help older women value themselves and see that their personal problems may be a result of societal sex, age, and race discrimination.

Jones, M. 1988. *Growing Old: The Ultimate Freedom.* New York: Human Sciences Press. The author shows how supportive and highly motivated peer groups can form the basis for freedom to change in old age.

Journal of Religion and Aging. 1984-1990; *Journal of Religious Gerontology.* 1991-present New York: Haworth Press. This quarterly, interdisciplinary journal of practice, theory, and applied research is a principal resource for the field.

Kaminisky, M. 1984. *The Uses of Reminiscence: New Ways of Working with Older Adults.* New York: Haworth Press. A coherent and sophisticated conceptual understanding of reminiscence. Several essays illustrate a variety of practical approaches for using reminiscence individually and in groups, to help participants accomplish a level of meaning that is personally integrative and socially critical.

Kimble, M., et al, eds. *The Aging, Religion, and Spirituality Handbook.* In press. A major work that will no doubt affect the field in substantial ways. Its 40 lengthy chapters cannot fail to mark the field both by content and by scope.

Levin, S. 1991. *Mingled Roots: A Guide for Jewish Grandparents of Interfaith Grandchildren.* Washington, DC: B'nai B'rith Women, 84 pp. Commissioned by B'nai B'rith Women in response to a need for support for grandparents, *Mingled Roots* serves as a loving "how to," offering specific suggestions to help grandparents share their Jewish heritage in ways that do not threaten their intermarried children.

Maitland, D. J. 1991. *Aging as Counterculture: A Vocation for the Later Years.* New York: Pilgrim. This book inquires into the distinctive possibilities in aging. The title of the book indicates clearly its thrust and dynamic.

Missinne, L. E. 1990. *Reflections on Aging: A Spiritual Guide.* Liguori, MO: Liguori. The book reflects on some fundamental questions of human existence in older age: meaning, suffering, purpose of living, Christian spirituality, aging, dying. Its particular emphasis is on the discovery of personal meaning in older age.

Myerhoff, B. 1984. "Rites and Signs of Ripening: The Intertwining of Ritual, Time, and Growing Older," in *Age and Anthropological Theory,* ed. D. I. Kertzer and J. Keith. Ithaca, NY: Cornell University Press. Myerhoff's seminal article is foundational for the development of rituals for aging in community.

Nouwen, J. and W. Gaffney. Photographs by Ron Van den Bosch. 1976. *Aging: The Fulfillment of Life.* New York: Doubleday. This photographic and spiritual essay on the meaning of aging emphasizes the need for inclusion so that despair—based on rejection by community and friends—will not overwhelm the inner self.

Older Adult Ministry: A Resource for Program Development. 1987. Atlanta: Presbyterian Publishing House. A loose-leaf guide for program development of nurturing ministries by and with older adults.

Pardue, L. 1991. "Models for Ministry: The Spiritual Needs of the Frail Elderly Living in Long-Term Care Facilities." *Journal of Religious Gerontology* 8(1): 13-24. Little information has been available pertaining to the spirituality of the institutionalized elderly. This paper presents the self-perceived spiritual needs of the elderly living in long-term care facilities.

Powers, E. A. 1988. *Aging Society: A Challenge to Theological Education.* Washington, DC: AARP. Papers written by scholars in eight disciplines central to theological education indicate what each discipline has to say about aging and being old in modern society, and ways to integrate aging information into the teaching of that discipline.

Richter, K., ed., and J. Simpson, comp. 1991. *Older Adult Ministry: A*

Guide for the Session and Congregation. Louisville, KY: Presbyterian Publishing House, 89 pp. This is the third volume in a series that includes *Older Adult Ministry: A Resource for Program Development,* available from the Episcopal Society for Ministry on Aging, and *Older Adult Ministry: A Guide for the Presbytery Committee.* All three volumes are of value.

Scannell, T., and A. Roberts. 1992. *State and Local Intergenerational Coalitions and Networks: A Compendium of Profiles.* Washington, DC: Generations United, 88 pp. This resource identifies 14 intergenerational coalitions and networks, with specifics about each.

Scott-Maxwell, F. 1979. *The Measure of My Days.* New York: Alfred A. Knopf. Extraordinarily perceptive personal reflections on aging, written at age 82 by an author and Jungian psychologist who views herself growing more passionate and intense with age. These reflections began as a notebook for asking and answering her own questions.

Sherman, E. 1991. *Reminiscence and the Self in Old Age.* New York: Springer, 272 pp. This benchmark study inquires about the various dimensions, types, and in-depth experiences of reminiscence and life review in old age. It is grounded in research and includes findings and ideas on a wide variety of topics associated with reminiscence.

Simmons, H. 1992. *In the Footsteps of the Mystics.* Mahwah, NJ: Paulist. Using a simple personality profile of four "ways" of spirituality, this book gathers writings from various authors (Jewish, Christian, Muslim, Native American), gathered around timeless human concerns.

Simmons, H., and V. Pierce, 1992. *Pastoral Responses to Older Adults and Their Families: An Annotated Bibliography.* New York: Greenwood. The first chapter, "Church and Synagogue," has seven subdivisions: comprehensive guides to ministry; specific programs and models; programs from particular perspectives; worship, ritual, preaching and hymns; educational programs for awareness and enrichment; social services; institutional care of the aged. Other chapters are "Empowerment"; "Ethics"; "Personal Spiritual Life"; "Life Review and Written Reminiscences"; "Death and Dying"; "Theology, Bible, and Other Religions"; "Religious Professionals"; "Special Populations"; and "Health and Religion." Since its publication in 1992, about 200 new items have been added. For those who have purchased the original volume, the update is available on disk (WP5.1) from H. Simmons, 1205 Palmyra Avenue, Richmond, VA 23227.

Stovich, R. J. 1988. *In Wisdom and Grace.* Kansas City, MO: Sheed and Ward. Creative and transforming images help older adults out of stagnation into growth, healing, and fulfillment. The style blends stories with insight from Jungian psychology and Christian faith.

Thibault, J. 1993. *A Deepening Love Affair with God in Late Life.* Nashville: Upper Room. This book is addressed to older adults who are spiritually restless and searching for a new depth in their relationship with God. The shift from greed to gift marks a radical turn toward God. Led by the Holy Spirit, older adults may become more sensitive to and appreciative of the gifts of old age and become more prepared for the work of taking a long, hard, honest look into the depths of mind and heart. This book is a theologically well-grounded, thoughtful companion on the journey of life in old age.

Tiso, F. V., ed. 1982. *Aging: Spiritual Perspectives.* Lake Worth, FL: Sunday Publications. This is one of the finest collections of articles on aging from a variety of religious perspectives: environmental, Native American, Hindu, Christian, Christian monastic, Buddhist, Islamic, Chinese, and Jewish. (Out of print, but available through interlibrary loan.)

Tully, M. and J. Turner. 1992. *Join the Club: Meeting the Special Needs of Men with Alzheimer's Disease.* (Join the Club, PO Box 40276, Washington, DC, 20016.) This "how to" guide for organizing a therapeutic program as an alternative or supplement to day care is based on a successful program sponsored by the Friends Meeting of Washington, DC. The club involves unimpaired retired volunteer peers (ages 65 to 85) who relate to the Alzheimer's members with respect, friendship, and camaraderie. The guide gives detailed instructions.